THE EVERYDAY ACTIVIST

EVERYTHING YOU NEED TO KNOW
TO GET OFF YOUR BACKSIDE
AND START TO MAKE A DIFFERENCE

MICHAEL NORTON

www.365act.com

Published with the collaboration of
UnLtd: The Foundation for Social Entrepreneurs

BOXTREE

First published 2007 by Boxtree
an imprint of Pan Macmillan Ltd
Pan Macmillan, 20 New Wharf Road, London N1 9RR
Basingstoke and Oxford
Associated companies throughout the world
www.panmacmillan.com

ISBN 978-0-7522-2635-4

9 8 7 6 5 4 3 2 1

A CIP catalogue record for this book is available from
the British Library.

Design and Illustration by Laugh it Off and Greenteabag
Design www.laughitoff.co.za and www.greenteabag.co.za

All photos provided by contributors unless stated otherwise.
Every effort has been made to contact uncredited copyright
holders of material reproduced in this book. If any have been
inadvertently overlooked, the publishers will be pleased to
make restitution at the earliest opportunity.

Printed and bound in Great Britain by
Butler & Tanner, Frome

Acknowledgements

The author wishes to thank all the people who are
featured in this book – who have actually gone out
and done something to help create a better world –
for allowing me to tell their amazing stories which
are an inspiration for the rest of us. My thanks
also to Penny Price from Boxtree for agreeing to
publish this book, and to Jon Butler for being a
sympathetic and helpful editor, to Justine Law for
helping me assemble case studies of some of the
UnLtd award winners. Mary Clemmey and Naimh
Walsh of the Mary Clemmey Literary Agency have
given me continuing encouragement and support.

Visit **www.panmacmillan.com** to read more about all our
books and to buy them. You will also find features, author
interviews and news of any author events, and you can sign
up for e-newsletters so that you're always first to hear about
our new releases.

"Change is not merely necessary to life; it *is* life."

ALVIN TOFFLER, *FUTURE SHOCK*

"Never doubt that a small group of thoughtful, committed citizens can change the world. Indeed, it is the only thing that ever has."

MARGARET MEAD, ANTHROPOLOGIST

"If you have nothing else to do, look about you and see if there isn't something close at hand that you can improve! It may make you wealthy, though it is more likely that it will make you happy."

GEORGE MATTHEW ADAMS,
NINETEENTH-CENTURY NEWSPAPER COLUMNIST
AND FONT OF POPULAR WISDOM

"How wonderful it is that nobody need wait a single minute before starting to improve the world."

ANNE FRANK, DIARIST AND HOLOCAUST VICTIM

READ THIS BOOK AND CHANGE THE WORLD

The theme of this book is that each and every one of us can do something to help make the world a better place. Through little things that we can do in our everyday lives and by taking action to address the issues that really concern us, we can all make a difference.

We should not leave it just to governments or to the big international organizations. Sure, both of these have an important role to play. But by taking action ourselves and coming up with our own solutions, we are showing that the public cares, which in turn puts pressure on those with more power and resources to treat the issues more seriously.

For example, the Make Poverty History campaign did not actually eliminate poverty. But it did draw attention to an important issue at the time of the G8 Summit in Gleneagles, Scotland, in July 2005, and encouraged world leaders to do something on trade, aid and debt for the world's poor. It urged all of us to write letters to world leaders telling them to take action. We could also listen to a Live 8 concert and buy a white wristband to show solidarity.

Poverty still persists, of course, and is likely to continue to do so. Although the problems are complex, there are, nevertheless, many things that we can do. For example, we could help every child receive an education by supporting the building and running of schools; we could

So if you believe that something needs doing, then do something.

Be creative. Come up with new and imaginative ways of doing things.

Enjoy what you are doing. Get excited about the difference that you are starting to make.

Encourage others to join in with you. Together, we can build a movement of active citizens who are determined to make the world a better place for all its inhabitants.

send a shoebox filled with school supplies to be used in the classroom; we could raise money to dig wells to bring clean water to people; we could purchase Fairtrade produce or buy crafts from local artisans. Everything we do can contribute towards making poverty history.

The beauty of small actions is that when lots and lots of people start doing lots and lots of things, then together we will make a huge difference.

HOW TO CHANGE THE WORLD

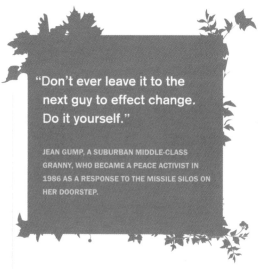

It's really quite easy. First, find out more about an issue that concerns you, an issue so important to you that you are prepared to put your time, your energy and even your money into doing something about it.

These might be some of the things that concern you:

- **Local issues** in your neighbourhood or community.
- Issues that **affect people of your age** – perhaps teen health as you are growing up, or pre-school education when you have children.
- Issues of **particular interest** to you and your friends – anything from Internet safety to stopping cruelty to animals or discouraging people from driving 4x4s.
- Issues that affect **your particular religious or ethnic group** – such as racism and discrimination.
- Issues that affect **your town or city** – such as poor public transport, a dirty river or summer smog.
- Issues that affect **your country** as a whole – such as the Iraq war or nuclear energy.
- **Global issues** – such as the destruction of the rainforest or Third World poverty.

Once you have decided what issues really concern you, you can:

- **Create your own solution.** Come up with a really interesting idea for what can be done to make things better.
- **Take action.** Do something. Start a project that addresses the problem. Invest your time and energy to make it work.
- **Get lots of publicity** and, in doing this, raise public awareness about the issue.
- Force **whoever is responsible** to take some sort of action to deal with it. Lobbying and arm-twisting can really work.
- **Encourage others** to do something. Persuade them that the issue is important. Suggest what they can do. Then help them get started.
- **Raise money,** which you can use for your own project or give to someone or some organization that is doing something.
- **Campaign** to get the law or the rules changed.

Just choose something you really care about . . . and get started. Don't hang around. Do it right now!

SIX STEPS TO CHANGING THE WORLD

Step 1: You can change the world [Page 12]

It's people who will make the world a bit better or their community a nicer place to live in. Everyone can play a part. Be inspired by some people who have gone out and done something. If they can do it, you can too. Find out if you have what it takes.

Step 2: Decide to become an everyday activist [Page 22]

Give up apathy. That's the biggest problem facing the world. Start by doing little things that will make a difference. Do lots of little things and you will begin to make a really big difference. Get into the habit of everyday activism. You will find that it will change you as well as change the world.

Step 3: What's the problem? [Page 44]

Now you're beginning to get into the swing of things. The next step is to identify the problems that are really important to you . . . in your life, in your community, in your country, in the wider world. What do you want to see made better? And are you prepared to do something about it?

Step 4: Come up with a solution [Page 68]

If there's a problem, there must also be a solution. Think creatively and come up with your very own world-beating idea for dealing with the problem. If you have a great idea, then making things happen becomes a whole lot easier.

Step 5: Go out and do something [Page 92]

Start your own project. Find others who will work with you to make something happen. It can be a lot of fun. You will make a difference, and you will make new friends. It could even change your life.

Step 6: World domination [Page 172]

Your project could become really successful. It could be replicated all over your country, perhaps even all over the world. You might even win a Right Livelihood Award or the Nobel Peace Prize. A great idea that meets a real need . . . oh, and a lot of hard work . . . that's all it takes!

THE ACTION GUIDE

To run a successful project, you need to be well organized, you need to tell people about what you are planning and what you have achieved, and you need to mobilize all the resources you will need. This book includes an action guide covering these three themes, each with examples and case studies, as well as twenty jam-packed pages giving practical advice on how to change the world.

Getting organized [Page 100]

Communication [Page 126]

Raising resources [Page 152]

HOW I BECAME AN ACTIVIST

Who am I?

My name is Michael Norton. I was born in London in 1942. I went to Cambridge University, where I gained a science degree. After university, I worked in merchant banking, and then in publishing. Today, I have grown-up children, and my hobbies include cycling and playing bridge.

How I became an activist:

On page [48], you will see that for many people there is often a "trigger point" which encourages them to get started. My trigger point was my father suggesting that I do some volunteering once I'd got my first job. I took him up on his "offer" and for the next two years spent my Monday nights at a youth club.

An inspiring story:

One of the things I did with the young people was to get them to visit the elderly after school. Two thirteen-year-olds told me with justifiable pride how they had taken a housebound old lady out for a walk. They had got hold of a wheelbarrow, filled it with cushions, assisted the old lady downstairs, and wheeled her around the block. The old lady was thrilled. It was the first time she'd been out for more than a year. I was amazed at the girls' ingenuity!

One thing led to another:

I saw myself as more of a follower than a leader, and I was terrified of speaking in public. But seeing that I could do something, encouraged me to do more – and by doing so, I started to change myself too. An issue I felt strongly about was the discrimination faced by newly arrived immigrants from the Caribbean and South Asia. I talked to friends who encouraged me to do something.

One skill I had was that I could speak English. So I decided to organize English classes in people's homes. I persuaded a few friends to become volunteer English teachers. I telephoned two schools in north-west London, and met the head teachers to ask if my idea for home tuition would be useful. They both said "Yes" and gave me the names and addresses of newly arrived students who might benefit.

I then knocked on doors and asked the family if they would let us come and give an English lesson one evening a week. Soon I had thirty volunteers teaching English in thirty homes . . . then it was fifty, then a hundred, and eventually over 200. We didn't need money to do it, we didn't have a bank account or even a name for the project. We were just a bunch of volunteers doing something that we all felt was important. It was a pioneering scheme in the UK, and it worked.

What I did next:

I enjoyed doing this more than going to work every day. So I decided to change career. My dream was to encourage people to go out and change the world for the better. In 1975, I founded the Directory of Social Change, which became the UK's largest provider of information and training to charities, helping them operate more effectively. I also wrote (and published) a number of books on fundraising. In 1995, I set up the Centre for Innovation in Voluntary Action to develop ideas for a better world. I have concentrated on user involvement, in encouraging young people to become "active citizens" and in the idea of "social entrepreneurship".

And what now?

I've written a book called *365 Ways to Change the World* which has lots of ideas for making a difference. And I'm also developing some of my own ideas, including MyBnk to promote young people's banking, carbon-neutral living on public housing estates, Neau bottled water *(see page 81),* and introducing the award-winning Canadian Otesha Project on sustainable living into the UK by encouraging young people to make the right "Morning Choices" *(see page 28).*

TO FIND OUT MORE ABOUT WHAT I AM UP TO, SEE

www.civa.org.uk and

www.365act.com

10
EASY THINGS
TO DO
RIGHT NOW

There's no point hanging about.
Every minute you fail to take action, more carbon dioxide is being pumped into the atmosphere, more acres of rainforest are being felled, more people are becoming HIV positive, more endangered languages are disappearing . . .

The time to get started is now! Here are ten simple things to do that *will* make a difference. Why not do all of them?

1 Go to the Rainforest site – click and donate

This is one of several sites where you can trigger a donation from the site's sponsor by clicking on an icon. Your click today will save one square metre of rainforest. It won't cost you a penny. Tomorrow you can save another square metre.
Go to **www.therainforestsite.com**

2 Collect your spare change

Get hold of a large jar to use as a collecting box. Every night empty your pockets of spare change. You decide which coins to keep for tomorrow and which to put in your collecting box. You will be amazed at how much you can collect without even noticing. Find a project that interests you, and donate your savings to it.

3 Change someone's life

If you're stuck for ideas, why not lend your money to help an entrepreneur in a developing country to help them set up a business? Quite a small amount of money can make a huge difference. And it's exciting to give your support directly to help one person. What's more, once they have made a success of their enterprise, they will repay your loan. You can then get your money back, or decide to lend it to somebody else.
Go to **www.kiva.org**

4 Fill a shoebox

Next time you buy a pair of shoes, keep the shoebox. Fill this up with educational supplies: pens, pencils, paper, notebooks, markers, rulers, whatever. You can give it, buy it, beg for it or even steal it. Then find someone who is going to a poor country where the schools just do not have enough money. Ask them to donate your shoebox to a school whilst they are there. This will help provide a class with a better education.

5 Give blood

Give blood and you could save a life. The hospital service needs blood for operations and emergencies. And whilst you're about it, become an organ donor and donate your body to medical research. If you don't know how to do any of this, ask your doctor.

6 Recycle your old spectacles

In the West we have the latest designer frames and two-pairs-for-the-price-of-one special offers. In the developing world, 200 million people live their lives in a haze of half-sight, too poor to have an eye test or buy a pair of spectacles. Your old specs could become a window to a bright new world for someone else. Donate your old spectacles. Start a collection in your community. Organizations such as Unite for Sight or Vision Aid Overseas will send them to where they're needed.

www.uniteforsight.org and
www.vao.org.uk

7 Lick global warming

We can all see the evidence of climate change around us: heatwaves, droughts, rising tides, melting glaciers, earlier seasons. World leaders have described global warming as "the single most important issue we face as a global community". But nothing will happen unless we do something. A first step is for you personally to pledge to reduce the carbon emissions you cause. Make a pledge right now to reduce your emissions by a tonne a year.

Go to **www.lickglobalwarming.org/pledge.cfm** to find out how.

8 Make a Good Gift

It's Christmas . . . or it's someone's birthday next week. And you don't know what to get them. Maybe they've got all they need. Maybe they never like what you choose. Here's the perfect answer. Buy a Good Gift. Their birthday gift is a goat for a widow in Rwanda. They'll really like it, as it will help transform someone's life. The even better news is that they won't have to look after the goat. The Good Gifts Catalogue is full of exciting gift ideas that will help change the world. See **www.goodgifts.org**

9 Link up your computer

You're hooked up to broadband. Most of the day your computer is doing nothing, when it could be helping solve an important problem – like the structure for an effective AIDS vaccine, or climate prediction that looks at the impact of global warming, or even whether extraterrestrial life exists. These problems are too large to be solved by one single computer. Enter the idea of distributed networks – thousands of computers all over the world working together to solve the problem when they would otherwise be idle. Join a distributed network.

Go to **www.distributedcomputing.info** and sign up for one of their active projects.

10 Join with others to change the world

On your own, you can do something. But with ninety-nine others, you will do a hundred times as much, and probably a lot more. This is where the PledgeBank comes in. You have an idea for changing the world. You make a pledge to do it – but only if other people pledge to do it too. When the required number of pledges have been received, all of you then do what you have promised. Put your own idea on the PledgeBank, or sign up to somebody else's pledge.

See **www.pledgebank.org**

Chapter 1

You can change the world

It's people who will make the world a bit better or their community a nicer place to live in. Everyone can play a part. Be inspired by some people who have gone out and done something. If they can do it, you can too. Find out if you have what it takes.

TWO PEOPLE WHO HAVE

The person: Rosa Parks, shop worker
The time: 1 December 1955, 6 pm
The place: Middle of a bus, downtown Montgomery, Alabama

After a day at work at Montgomery Fair department store, forty-two-year-old Rosa Parks boarded the Cleveland Avenue bus, paid her fare and sat in an empty seat in the front row of seats in the 'colored section' near the middle of the bus and directly behind the ten seats reserved for whites. As the bus proceeded, all the whites-only seats filled up. At the Empire Theater stop, several more white passengers boarded.

In 1900, Montgomery had passed a city ordinance for the purpose of segregating passengers by race. Bus drivers had adopted the practice of requiring black passengers to move whenever there were no whites-only seats left. Following standard practice, the bus driver moved the 'colored section' sign behind Parks and demanded that four black people give up their seats to white passengers. Three complied, but Rosa Parks stayed seated.

The driver then said, "Why don't you stand up?" Parks replied, "I don't think I should have

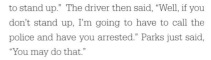

> "People always say that I didn't give up my seat because I was tired, but that isn't true . . . no, the only tired I was, was tired of giving in."
>
> ROSA PARKS

to stand up." The driver then said, "Well, if you don't stand up, I'm going to have to call the police and have you arrested." Parks just said, "You may do that."

Rosa Parks was charged with disorderly conduct and violating a local ordinance, found guilty, and fined $10 plus $4 court costs.

On 5 December 1955, about a dozen or more people gathered to discuss what to do. They formed the Montgomery Improvement Association to lead a boycott of Montgomery's buses, and elected Dr Martin Luther King Jr as their President. He was then a young and largely unknown minister of Dexter Avenue Baptist Church.

Standing up for what you believe in isn't always easy. For Rosa Parks it was her refusal to stand up in the face of what she saw as a fundamental injustice that sparked the Civil Rights Movement which changed the face of the United States of America.

Rosa Parks went on to found the Rosa and Raymond Parks Institute for Self-Development. When Rosa Parks died in October 2005, her body lay in state at the US Capitol (she was only the thirty-first person and the first woman to be accorded this honour).

www.Rosaparks.org
http://en.wikipedia.org/wiki/Rosa_Parks

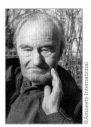

©Amnesty International

The person: Peter Benenson, lawyer
The time: November 1960
The place: St Martin-in-the-Fields, London

"Only when the last prisoner of conscience has been freed, when the last torture chamber has been closed, when the United Nations' Universal Declaration of Human Rights is a reality for the world's people, will our work be done."

PETER BENENSON

15

In 1960, Portugal was ruled by the dictator Antonio Salazar. Two Portuguese students had just been sentenced to seven years' imprisonment for the seemingly trivial act of raising their glasses in a toast to freedom in a Lisbon cafe.

A thirty-nine-year-old British lawyer, Peter Benenson, had read about this in the *Daily Telegraph* on his way to work. Educated at Eton and Oxford, a wartime code-breaker, and a co-founder of Justice, which promotes human rights and law reform in the UK, Benenson was so outraged that he went into St Martin-in-the-Fields church and sat down for forty-five minutes to think things over. He came up with the idea of trying to free prisoners of conscience by organizing letter-writing campaigns.

Benenson contacted David Astor, editor of the *Observer*, who offered him the front-page for an article. This appeared on 28 May 1961. It began with these words: "Open your newspaper any day of the week and you will find a report from somewhere in the world of someone being imprisoned, tortured or executed because his opinions or religion are unacceptable to his government. There are several million such people in prison – by no means all of them behind the Iron and Bamboo Curtains – and their numbers are growing. The newspaper

reader feels a sickening sense of impotence. Yet if these feelings of disgust could be united into common action, something effective could be done.

"We have set up an office in London to collect information about the names, numbers and conditions of what we have decided to call Prisoners of Conscience, and we define them thus: Any person who is physically restrained (by imprisonment or otherwise) from expressing (in any form of words or symbols) an opinion which he honestly holds and which does not advocate or condone personal violence." Benenson proposed a twelve-month "Amnesty" campaign of letter-writing. The response was overwhelming – with over 1,000 offers of support.

This was the birth of Amnesty International. Within a year letter-writing groups had formed in over a dozen countries. Today, Amnesty is the world's largest human rights organization with nearly 2 million members worldwide. In 1977, Amnesty won the Nobel Peace Prize for its human rights work.

www.amnesty.org
http://en.wikipedia.org/wiki/Peter_Benenson

An old Quaker proverb says: "It is better to light a single candle than to curse the darkness."

Are you someone who will light that candle?

Or will you continue to moan that things could be better, without doing anything about it?

What sort of person becomes a change-maker?

Special people, extraordinary people, who are born with the leadership skills, the creativity, the energy, the ambition and the social values that will be needed to be successful leaders of change?

or

Ordinary people (like you and me) who decide to do something about a problem or issue they care about? Then by doing this, and by learning from our mistakes as well as our successes, we develop new skills and our self-confidence begins to grow. We may then go on to do more and bigger things, and become extraordinary in the process.

The truth probably lies somewhere between the two extremes. There are exceptional people; but even ordinary people can do extraordinary things if they really want to.

It is taking the first step which is crucial – deciding that something needs doing and that you are the person who will do something about it.

Once you get going, you will learn from experience and gain confidence from your successes. You will develop all the qualities you need to succeed as you go along.

In this book you will read stories of people who have taken that first step. Some are young – the youngest is just six years old. Some are nearing the end of their lives. Most are in between. Their stories should inspire us and show us that if we feel strongly enough about an issue or a problem and are prepared to "give it a go", then a better world is possible.

HAVE YOU GOT WHAT IT TAKES?

It is interesting to speculate about *"What if . . ."*, about what the world would be like if something *hadn't* happened.

For example, *what if* Rosa Parks hadn't been the one who refused to give up her seat? How and when would the US Civil Rights movement have started?

Or, *what if* Peter Benenson hadn't been so outraged by what had happened to the two Portuguese students that he had gone straight into work instead of walking into a church? When would the world have woken up to the plight of prisoners of conscience?

It takes just one person to create change. A person who thinks that things do not have to stay just as they are, but that they could be and should be better; a person who is also prepared to go and do something about it – even if this is something quite small to start with.

IF A CHILD OF SIX CAN DO IT...

When Groucho Marx was told that something was so simple that even a child of five could understand it, he famously replied: "Then fetch me a child of five!" Here is the true and inspiring story of how six-year-old Ryan started building wells in Africa.

Ryan Hreljac comes from Kemptville, Ontario, in Canada. When he was six, his teacher, Mrs Prest, told the class that there were many people in Africa who did not have access to clean drinking water, and who were constantly sick and even dying as a result. Ryan was speechless. He couldn't understand how some people on the planet could be without water, whilst for him it was a simple matter of turning on the tap. He learned, however, that a well could be built in one of the places where water was desperately needed for just $70.

When Ryan got home, he went straight to his parents and said, "Mom, Dad, can I have seventy dollars?" Not surprisingly, they said "No." But they did agree to help him find ways of raising the money. By doing extra chores around the house for his parents and his neighbours for four months, Ryan eventually raised the $70 he needed. He took the money to WaterCan, a Canadian non-profit charity which provides water in developing countries. He even brought an extra $5 to pay for lunches for the people who would be building the well.

The people at WaterCan were, of course, greatly inspired by Ryan's determination and enthusiasm. But they had to tell him that it actually cost $2,000 to build a well. "No problem," Ryan replied, "I'll just do more chores then." News of Ryan spread quickly throughout his community and soon people started to send money to Ryan to assist him. Before long Ryan had raised enough money to build his first well.

Six months later, in January 1999, Canadian Physicians for Aid and Relief drilled "Ryan's Well" beside the Angolo Primary School in northern Uganda. When Ryan was given the opportunity to see his well, the experience changed his life more than he had ever expected. Being there caused him to realize that he could do even more.

After many years of hard work Ryan's Well Foundation was established in 2001. By the end of 2006, the then fifteen-year-old Ryan and his organization had raised over $1.5 million and completed 266 water and sanitation projects in twelve countries helping over 435,000 people. And the effort continues. "I'm just a normal boy," says Ryan when asked about his achievements. Many would disagree.

Ryan speaks across Canada and internationally at schools, clubs, universities and conferences, promoting the message that people everywhere should have a right to clean water . . . and showing through his personal example how one person can make a huge difference. If a child of six can do it, then so can you.

www.ryanswell.ca

Spot the difference...

Here's another story of a child who was inspired to do something, which also happened in 1999. Ten-year-old Ho heard about the poverty that many young children were experiencing in his own country, Vietnam. It was just after the Tet festival when it is traditional for children to receive gifts of money. Ho decided to send his Tet money to the National Foundation for Children in Hanoi asking that it be spent to benefit less-advantaged children. The Foundation wrote a polite letter of thanks. And that was that.

What a missed opportunity! If Ho felt like this, then there must be tens of thousands of other young people who felt similarly and who could emulate Ho's example.

A bit of publicity, a national campaign launched by the Foundation and fronted by Ho could have developed into something similar to a Ryan's Well, inspiring the young people of Vietnam to action. It wasn't Ho's fault. He did what he felt he had to. But often people just can't see that there is a huge opportunity to make a difference. With a bit of help from the National Foundation, Ho could have become Vietnam's answer to Ryan. (Based on a true story.)

ROB THE RUBBISH

This is the story of how one man addressed an everyday problem, and decided to do something about it, rather than moan.

Robin Kevan is a sixty-one-year-old retired social worker. What was irking him was litter. He had always **seen** litter, but had never really **noticed** it. After he retired, he began to notice it everywhere as he walked in some of the country's most beautiful places. Some people would just grumble that the streets were very dirty and castigate those that cause it. Others might want to ring up the Council and ask them to do something about it. Always passing the buck. Not Rob. He decided to do something himself. He decided to pick it up on the basis that once litter has been removed it can no longer offend anyone and the beauty behind it can be seen.

Almost every day, Rob goes out first thing in the morning in the tiny Welsh town of Llanwrtyd Wells (which happens to be the smallest town in Britain) to pick up litter. Armed with the simplest of equipment – gloves, a pick-up stick, yellow jacket and black bin bags – he does what's needed.

Not content with just this, he also decided to clean up the countryside around his home picking up the litter left on the surrounding Cambrian Mountains and Brecon Beacons.

His litter-picking activity got publicity in the national press. Word began to spread. He became known as "Rob the Rubbish" and is now known throughout the world for what he does. He regularly cleans up other mountains and beautiful places, amongst which are not only the UK's highest mountains, Ben Nevis, Snowdon and Scafell Pike but also the Everest base camp trail in Nepal – which must count as "the peak" of his mission to make the world a cleaner place.

Rob started as one man with time on his hands. He used that time with courage, determination and energy to do something about a problem that was annoying him. He is inspired by the impact he is having and in turn inspires others. He believes that the biggest problems can sometimes have the simplest of solutions and unexpected spin-offs.

Rob is at the other end of the age spectrum from Ryan. He is a shining example of a "just-do-it" and "change the world" ethos that can inspire us all.

www.robtherubbish.com

SOMETIMES YOU JUST HAVE TO DO SOMETHING

"Sometimes you just have to do something, don't you? Sometimes an injustice comes along and you think: 'No, this cannot be', and rather than just turn off the TV, you know it's time to act."

This is how Isabel Losada began her book *A Beginner's Guide to Changing the World.*

Isabel was a single mum, living in Battersea. She wanted to bring to public attention the way in which governments were fighting violence with more violence whilst ignoring one of the world's greatest living proponents of peace – the Dalai Lama. She wanted to explore what impact she herself could make. She used as her framework the famous prayer *"Grant me the Serenity to accept what I can't change, the Courage the change the things I can, and the Wisdom to know the difference."*

She had never done anything like this before, but she set about her task with optimism and fearlessness. Over the next year she would:

- Travel to Tibet to research her subject.

- Support the Free Tibet Campaign by attending a BP shareholders' meeting dressed as a Chinese soldier to ironically applaud the company's investment in Petro-China.

- Enjoy fundraising by jumping out of an aeroplane.

- Take tea with the Chinese Ambassador and question him about the Dalai Lama and Tibetan autonomy. He was not amused.

- Hang a 15-metre banner from Nelson's Column with a picture of the Dalai Lama, and get a base jumper to jump from the top (which ensured international media attention).

- Interview the Dalai Lama about how one person can make a difference.

- Write a bestselling book about all of this.

Inspired by her book, thousands of people took action. They sponsored the education of Tibetan children, volunteered in Tibet, provided healthcare for former prisoners, supported the training of midwives, supported small health projects for Tibetan nomads, and kept the question of China's treatment of Tibet as a constant pressure on the UK Foreign office.

Isabel's 10 indispensable things for changing the world:

1. A storage cupboard – to put your TV in.
2. A crazy, wonderful, joyful, positive plan.
3. Selective deafness (complete inability to hear the word "No" or "Can't" or "That's a bad idea").
4. A coffee addiction – it's impossible otherwise.
5. Unconditional love for others 24/7 – this is essential.
6. Deranged friends to help you.
7. An irrational desire to do mad things (such as jump out of planes), sometimes called fundraising.
8. A website that you make and maintain yourself.
9. An unbalanced sense of humour.
10. Persistence.

see www.actfortibet.com

Chapter 2

Decide to become an everyday activist

Give up apathy. That's the biggest problem facing the world. Start by doing little things that will make a difference. Do lots of little things and you will begin to make a really big difference. Get into the habit of everyday activism. You will find that it will change you as well as change the world.

GIVE UP APATHY

What is the biggest problem facing the world today? Is it HIV/AIDS? Is it global warming? Is it poverty and inequality in the world? Is it environmental degradation? No. It's none of these. The world's biggest problem is apathy – that too few people are prepared to do anything about all these and other problems. CYNDI RHOADES

Cyndi Rhoades was born near vast corn fields in the capital city of Columbus, Ohio. She moved to London in 1992. Her career began as a film producer and director of music videos. As her personal interests began to broaden in her mid-twenties, she moved into more factual film-making.

"The more I learned about what was going on in the world the more I wanted to do something about it. My personal trigger point was reading David Korten's When Corporations Rule the World. This totally sparked my passion. So many injustices – corruption, climate change, poverty and inequality – yet we all seem to be sitting around doing nothing about it."

Cyndi started asking her friends why they were doing nothing. The general response was, "It's not that I don't care. It's just that the problems are too big and beyond my reach. How can anything that one person does actually make a difference? Why bother?"

She approached the New Economics Foundation (a think tank that turns ideas into action) with an idea. Anti-Apathy would provide a mechanism for getting people to understand more about the part they can play in shaping the world and bringing about positive social and environmental change.

The original concept for Anti-Apathy was to combine a panel of respected speakers on a particular topic and show short films, play live music and, of course, provide beer in a nightclub setting – to create an atmosphere where people would feel comfortable and engaged. The focus was on looking at what's really behind our day-to-day lives, from the clothes we wear to the food we eat. People loved the events; and they wanted more.

Anti-Apathy has now blossomed into an independent organization which is more than just evening events. It includes social experiments, online action campaigns and the Worn Again fashion label *(see page 82)*. The aim is to help people turn from being passive to active citizens, and to show how individual actions can make a difference and how change can come if enough people demand it.

www.antiapathy.org

THE TWELVE-STEP ANTI-APATHY RECOVERY PLAN

Recovering from apathy and its effects can seem a long and arduous journey, but Anti-Apathy is here to help. Anti-Apathy has developed a "scientifically tested" (well, kind of) voluntary programme to personal recovery from the adverse effects of apathy. Try it.

Step 1:

Admit that there is a problem and that *a life addicted to apathy is a life half lived.*

Step 2:

Repeat the following until you believe it: *"The power to change things and restore society lies within each and every one of us."*

Step 3:

Ponder the question, *"What can I do?"* (And while you're at it, list some answers.)

Step 4:

Make a list of *all the practices in your everyday life* that stress the planet, society and your wellbeing.

Step 5:

Act on your discoveries.

Step 6:

Hug a tree. If it is too wide, mobilize your community to link arms, and then together hug the aforementioned tree.

Step 7:

Reject the doctrine of individualism and see the world as an interdependent whole.

Step 8:

Learn a new joke.

Step 9:

Befriend a politician (let's face it most of them could do with at least one).

Step 10:

Tell your new joke to a stranger on the street and your new politician friend.

Step 11:

Having experienced a spiritual awakening as the result of these steps, *carry this message of hope to other apathetics.*

Step 12:

Ignore all of this. Find your own path to recovery.

Note: If you don't know any jokes, subscribe free to receive A-Joke-A-Day via a monthly e-mail; some are actually funny.

www.ajokeaday.com

"You must be the
change you wish
to see in the world."

MAHATMA GANDHI

BE THE CHANGE

**The life of Mahatma Gandhi should
inspire every activist.**

Gandhi studied law in England. In 1893 as a young lawyer, he moved to South Africa where he experienced racial discrimination, which was then commonplace in the daily lives of blacks, coloureds and Indians.

He was thrown off a train after refusing to move from the first class to a third class coach while holding a valid first class ticket. Then taking a stagecoach, he was beaten by a driver for refusing to travel on the footboard to make room for a European passenger. He suffered other hardships on the journey, including being barred from many hotels.

Gandhi responded by becoming a leading campaigner for civil rights for Indians in South Africa. In 1894, he founded the Natal Indian Congress. In 1914, he returned to India to fight for his country's independence.

Gandhi revolutionized social action through the tactics he developed – which included mass civil disobedience with a commitment to non-violence.

In India, Gandhi was imprisoned and went on hunger strike several times. His most famous protest was the Salt March to Dandi in 1930. He and thousands of Indians marched 400 kilometres to the Gujarat coast to produce their own salt from seawater, a symbolic act of protest against the British monopoly on salt production and the high taxes they were levying on this essential commodity. In 1947, largely as a result of Gandhi's leadership, India achieved independence.

LEARN MORE ABOUT GANDHI
www.mkgandhi.org

Read *'Nonviolence: 25 lessons from the history of a dangerous idea'* by Mark Kurlansky.

Learn the techniques of non-violent protest by going on an action training camp organized by the Ruckus Society

www.ruckus.org

BECOME AN EVERYDAY ACTIVIST

Change has to start somewhere and with someone. It started with Gandhi when he decided that he would simply not accept being treated as a second-class citizen in South Africa. It can also start with **you**, when you decide that something is unacceptable, that you won't put up with it any longer.

Whatever the problem that concerns you – whether it's freedom from oppression or international poverty or global warming or poor public transport or "hoodies" roaming the streets – be the person who decides to do something.

There are also lots of little things that you can do every day in your own life, with your family, at your workplace and in your community which will help make the world a better place. Begin to incorporate some of these everyday actions into how you live your life.

Be inspired by Gandhi. Be the change you wish to see in the world.

Some other quotes from Gandhi:

"Whatever you do may seem insignificant to you, but it is most important that you do it."

"First they ignore you, then they laugh at you, then they fight you, then you win."

"Non-violence is the greatest force at the disposal of mankind. It is mightier than the mightiest weapon of destruction devised by the ingenuity of man."

"There are many causes that I am prepared to die for but no causes that I am prepared to kill for."

CHANGE THE WORLD THIS MORNING

Before you start to think about changing the world, start thinking about the choices you make each day as you go about your daily life.

In the everyday things you do – at home and at work – you can continue to do things the way you are doing them now, which may be doing little to help make a better world. Or you could do exactly the same things in a completely different way, in a way that will help create positive change.

For example, your morning caffeine fix – you can buy Fairtrade coffee, which will ensure that the growers earn a decent living from their efforts. If you pick up a coffee at Starbucks on your way to work, you can take your own china mug along with you, rather than have to drink it from a disposable cardboard or styrofoam cup. Or you could buy a cafetiere and make your own when you get to work – and then donate the money you save to help reduce poverty and inequality.

Each of these simple choices will help save resources and contribute to a fairer world. Each will make a small difference. Getting into the habit of making positive choices will make

you conscious that you actually can make a difference to the world through your everyday actions.

Taking the message out – even if it means cycling 5,500 miles

Two twenty-one-year-old Canadian students, Jocelyn Land-Murphy and Jessica Lax, met in 2002 on a gap year in Kenya. Their experience of poverty highlighted for them the huge difference between their lives and expectations and the much more restricted opportunities that were available to people in the developing world. It raised the question of the mindless overconsumption in the rich world.

They wanted to bring these issues down to a personal level. This meant first a change in attitude, which in turn would lead to making changes in their own lives. They also saw that they could have a much bigger impact if they could take this message out to Canada's youth. So in February 2002 on a beautiful sunny day sitting under a tree in Kenya, they decided to create the Otesha Project. Otesha means "Reason to Dream" in Kiswahili.

Fourteen months later, they made their dream a reality. They got together a group of thirty-three volunteers and cycled over 5,500 miles in 164 days and made over 250 presentations to more than 12,000 young Canadians.

The Otesha Project has organized cycle tours every year since then. In 2006, Jocelyn and Jessica were awarded an international prize for what they had achieved.

> "We know that everything we do has an impact on the world, and because we truly want a sustainable future, we question every single one of our personal actions. We try, with every action, to minimize the negative and to maximize the positive."
>
> **JOCELYN LAND-MURPHY AND JESSICA LAX**

FIND OUT MORE ABOUT THE OTESHA PROJECT AND DOWNLOAD *THE OTESHA HANDBOOK:*

www.otesha.ca

"From getting dressed, to grabbing a coffee, to transporting ourselves to school or work, we know that we can either be contributing to child labour, exploitation of people and land, pollution and climate change, OR we can contribute to alternative income projects, fair trade and sustainable agriculture, and an emissions-free bicycle culture. The change we make in the world is up to us."

JOCELYN LAND-MURPHY AND JESSICA LAX

29

Jocelyn and Jessica's brilliant idea was that we can change our lives *for just one hour of the day* (between 8.00 and 9.00am), and by doing this we can begin to change the whole world.

On the next three pages, you can see some of the "Morning Choices" that you can think about making...

MORNING CHOICES...

Morning Choices: The water you use

The amount of water in the world is limited, and 20 per cent of the world's population does not have access to safe drinking water. After global warming, water is the world's next most serious problem. From London to Los Angeles, supply is exceeding demand. *Do one of these today:*

- Cut down on your water use. Have a shorter shower; or share your bath with a friend – or at least the bathwater.

- Mind what you put into your water. Buy eco-detergents and recycled loo paper.

- Drink tap water not bottled water. Fill up an empty bottle and so save on congestion and pollution.

Morning Choices: The clothes you wear

Much of the cheap clothing we crave is made by poor people in poor countries working in sweatshop conditions. Growing cotton consumes tonnes of water, often in water-stressed regions. *Do one of these today:*

- Buy less, wear more. And make sure what you buy is sweatshop free.

- Buy T-shirts that are hemp-cotton mix.

- Go through your wardrobe, and take your old clothes into a charity shop. Whilst you are there take a look at their stock, and see if there's anything you like the look of.

Construct a simple toilet

Architect Andrej Pretnar, who is Slovenian, has designed a simple toilet, using buckets and other waste materials which you can construct in fifteen minutes. This survival skill will take just an hour to learn. The toilet will need to be emptied only once a week (based on 0.25 litre of water for each flushing), and it can be connected to a bidet or a washbasin to reuse water. It can then be converted into a chemical toilet or latrine. Andrej's website gives instructions. A free CD-ROM with a video showing the assembly procedure and operation is also available.

www.studio.moj.net

Morning Choices: The breakfast you eat

A healthy balanced diet is one key to wellbeing. But even if you eat well, there is an environmental impact.
Do one of these today:

• Buy local and buy seasonal. Check the label and cut down on your food miles. Go shopping at your local farmer's market and support local independent shops whenever you can.

• Eat organic. Join a box scheme, and get a box of organic vegetables delivered once a week. Do this to reduce the chemicals that you and the environment are exposed to.

• Buy Fairtrade whenever you can. Tea, coffee, sugar, honey, chocolate, fruit, snack bars. Doing this will ensure a better deal for the producers.

Morning Choices: The energy you use

Energy use in the home is a major contributor to global warming. Use less energy, and you will not only save money, but you will also help save the world!
Do one of these today:

• Switch to Green Electricity. You can do this at no extra cost. See www.uswitch.com

• Turn down the heating by 1 degree, and adjust the time switch to align more closely with the time you spend at home.

• Turn off your TV and your computer whenever you finish using it. Don't leave your equipment on stand-by.

Free coffee from Starbucks

Starbucks uses a lot of coffee. But they then have a problem about what to do with the coffee grounds. Rather than seeing this as waste and throwing it away, they bag up the used grounds to give away to customers to use as fertilizer.

Coffee grounds have a high nitrogen content but are slightly acidic.

Mixed with dry leaves to balance the acidity, they can then be used to:

• Enrich your garden soil so you can grow prize-winning marrows.

• Turn on the heat to speed up your composting.

• Give a caffeine high to the worms in your vermi-composter.

If there isn't a Starbucks near you, go and talk to other coffee chains, hotels, fast- food outlets and other mega-users of coffee. Your own Fairtrade coffee grounds will work equally well!

STARBUCKS AND COMPOSTING:
www.starbucks.com/aboutus/compost.asp

Morning Choices: The waste you create

Disposing of rubbish is a major problem as landfills fill up. The answer is the three Rs: Reduce, Reuse and Recycle. *Do one of these today:*

- Buy a sturdy cloth or hessian bag. Take this with you when you go shopping; use this instead of the free plastic bags that are offered at the checkout.

- Start composting your kitchen waste. Order worms from www.wigglywigglers.co.uk

- Switch to using reusable batteries. But also recycle your used batteries, rather than throwing them away. Get a tin or a box which you will use to store them before you dispose of them. Find out more from http://ehso.com/battery.php

- Organize a collection of used toner cartridges at your workplace (or at school or college) and turn these into cash for your chosen charity. See www.emptycartridge.co.uk

Morning Choices: The way you travel

Along with home energy use, transport is the other major contributor to global warming. Cut down on your transport emissions. *Do one of these today:*

- Walk to school or work today. Use shoe rubber, not tyre rubber. Find out the best route at www.walkit.com (available in central London only at the moment).

- Go and get a bicycle. Keep fit whilst you whiz through the congestion.

- Next time you travel by road, use www.liftshare.org to share your journey or to find someone travelling to where you want to go.

- Pledge to fly less. Make a "gold pledge" where you undertake not to take any flights for one year. Or a silver pledge where you will take not more than two return short-haul flights, or one return long-haul flight in the next year. www.flightpledge.org.uk

Take back the packaging

The Women's Institute is gaining a reputation for radicalism. Not only did the Rylstone and District branch produce the original Calendar Girls nude calendar for 2000 to raise money for cancer research (on which the film starring Helen Mirren was based), but in June 2006, they organized a national day of action when members were asked to return excess packaging to the supermarkets where they had bought the food.

Foods such as fruits and vegetables are being packaged unnecessarily – shrink-wrapped cucumbers and coconuts, bananas in plastic bags, apples and courgettes on plastic trays. Most of this packaging is non-recyclable. More than 4.6 million tonnes has to be disposed of each year. Do what the Women's Institute members did. Ask the supermarkets to improve their environmental policies on packaging and foodwaste..

www.womens-institute.co.uk/campaigns/packagingday.shtml

DOING MY BIT FOR GLOBAL WARMING

My name is Kyla Davis. I am twenty-five and live in London. Having trained at the School of Physical Theatre I am an actress by profession. As a committed environmentalist, I am concerned about climate change.

Since 2003, I have been working with a charity called Save our World to develop an educational show for children. The Climate Change Roadshow was first presented at green fairs around London and then at elementary schools in Lambeth. The show consists of a performance followed by an interactive workshop about energy efficiency, specifically about how our daily choices affect the world's climate.

I am also a trustee of Save our World and an online member of organizations such as Greenpeace, Friends of the Earth, Campaign Against Climate Change and Stop Climate Chaos.

This is what I am doing about global warming in my own life:

- I reduce, reuse, refill, repair, recycle everything that I can. I refill used jars and containers, repair things before throwing them away, shop only at charity/second hand shops, carry my own reusable shopping bags, reuse paper and envelopes.
- I wash at 30 degrees and avoid tumble dryers and dishwashers.
- I shower instead of having a bath.
- I bought a bicycle and I try to cycle or walk everywhere.
- I compost my organic waste.
- When I'm cold I put on more clothes rather than turn up the heating.
- I have only energy-efficient light bulbs.
- I switched my energy provider to renewable energy.
- I switch off all appliances at the wall and turn off things I'm not using. I sometimes do this to other people's appliances (guerrilla tactics!).
- I write to my MP and the Prime Minister

urging them to take drastic action to avert climate change.

- I no longer fly.
- I went on a climate change speaker training day, so I can now talk publicly about the issue. Log on to www.coinet.org.uk if you want to do this.
- I have joined a number of online groups and attend lectures, talks, debates and seminars to get up-to-date information.

Things that I want to do in the future:

- Grow my own food using permaculture principles, and eventually become self-sufficient.
- To stop eating out so much and buying takeaway sandwiches and coffees.
- To live in a house that is completely carbon neutral with solar panels and wind turbines, and eventually to help build a cooperative, carbon-neutral community.
- To discuss, argue and debate climate change with as many people as possible to convert them into believing that they can do their bit to save the planet.

60
WAYS TO
SAVE THE
ENVIRONMENT

Turning the tap off when you brush your teeth or putting a bird box in your garden may not solve the problems of the world by themselves, but there are lots of little things like these that you can do which will certainly help.

The UK's Environment Agency came up with sixty ideas to mark World Environment Day 2004 **www.environment-agency.gov.uk/wed**

Clean air:

1. Drive less

2. Drive smart – accelerate gradually, obey speed limits, combine several errands in one trip

3. Limit how long your car engine runs when you've stopped

4. On cold days, wait to start the engine until just before you move off

5. Use a car with a three-way catalytic converter

Pollution and wildlife:

6. Put out a bird feeder or nesting box

7. Support local wildlife organizations

8. Build a pond in your garden

9. Don't be a litterbug

10. Support community litter clean-ups

11. Put your rubbish out just before collection time

12. Take part in a local tree-planting scheme

13. Buy products made from sustainably produced wood

Water:

14. Take showers not baths

15. Limit use of garden sprinklers or hoses

16. Use a bucket to wash your car

17. Use a nappy washing service

18. Choose plants that don't need much water

19. Collect rain water

20. Put a bag of water in your lavatory cistern to reduce the water flushed

21. Turn the tap off when brushing your teeth

22. Use full loads in your dishwasher and washing machine

23. Check new appliances are water-efficient

24. Repair dripping taps and turn taps off properly

25. Use environmentally friendly cleaning products

26. Don't put oil, paint, varnish or solvent down the drain

27. Don't put sanitary products, nappies or cigarettes down the loo

Energy use:

28. Use green energy

29. Get energy saving tips from your supplier

30. Buy local produce or grow your own

31. Fly less, much less

32. Check new appliances for energy efficiency

33. Use thermostats that switch off the heating when you're out

34. Insulate your home

35. Use a fan instead of air conditioning

36. Turn off appliances and lights when not needed

37. Fit energy-efficient light bulbs

38. Heat small meals in a microwave

39. Insulate your hot water tank properly

40. Dry your clothes on a clothes line

Waste:

41. Use a doorstep recycling scheme

42. . . . or ask for one to be started

43. Send e-cards at Christmas

44. Buy products made from recycled materials

45. Choose products with recycled packaging

46. Make your own compost

47. Re-use plastic shopping bags or use cloth bags

48. Use plastic storage boxes not foil or wrap

49. Use rechargeable batteries

50. Print and photocopy on both sides of paper

51. Reuse envelopes – cross out the old address

52. Prolong tyre life by maintaining the correct pressure

53. Find people to use the things you no longer want

54. Use a cloth hankie rather than tissues

55. Avoid using disposable items

56. Use the front of greeting cards to create postcards or gift tags

57. Ask hotels not to change sheets and towels daily

58. Cook fresh food (which has less packaging)

59. Donate leftover paint to a community project

60. Drink tap or filtered water, not bottled

Go through this list and pledge to do at least twenty of these things . . . more if you can.

BE AN ETHICAL CONSUMER

Make your money talk. Make ethical choices in what you buy and from whom you buy. Bank with an ethical bank. Buy Fairtrade.

Here is what the active consumer can do to address the issue of unfair trade:

1. Buy Fairtrade tea, coffee, bananas, chocolate. Buy a Fairtrade football and kick it around. Enjoy!

2. Buy Fairtrade presents for your friends. And ask them to switch.

3. Order Fairtrade coffee whenever you go out for a coffee. If you have to pay extra, try to find out how much of the extra actually goes to the growers. Write to the company for an answer if the staff can't tell you.

4. Become a *Dubble agent.* Go to your local newsagent or sweet shop, and ask if they stock Dubble or other Fairtrade chocolate brands. Check the amount of stock and where it is displayed. Ask the shop owner to order more and display it more prominently.

5. Get your workplace to buy Fairtrade tea, coffee and biscuits. Or even install a Fairtrade vending machine for snacks and drinks.

6. Don't buy Fairtrade if it's too expensive. Just donate the extra you would be paying to support people's livelihoods in the developing world. This could do even more good.

7. Organize a "mad hatter's tea-party", with fancy hats and Fairtrade tea, to raise money for international development.

8. Campaign to get your town declared a "Fairtrade Town" (to promote fairly traded foods) or a "Sweat-free City" (to stop the sale of goods produced in sweat shops). There are also "Transition Towns" (which encourage people to buy local) and "Slow Cities" (to slow down the pace of life, and concentrate on enjoyment).

Check out these websites

Ethical Consumer: www.ethicalconsumer.org

Fair Trade: www.fairtrade.org.uk

Mad Hatter's Tea Party: www.coffeebreak.org.uk

Fairtrade towns: http://en.wikipedia.org/wiki/Fairtrade_Town

Slow cities: www.cittaslow.org.uk

Sweat-free cities: www.sweatfree.org

Transition towns: www.transitiontowns.org

START LOCAL

There's a lot you can do not just to sort out local problems and to create a sense of pride in your neighbourhood. Here are ten simple ideas for the everyday activist:

1. Brighten up the street. Decorate your house or garden or balcony with an amazing array of lights (low energy, of course) and figures at Christmas-time.

2. Become a guerrilla gardener*. Plant your seeds out. Water them with love. Watch them come into flower.

3. Remove eyesores. Paint over graffiti or create a mural. Remove some detritus that has been dumped (or just telephone your local Council and tell them to do it).

4. Don't ignore the homeless. They're as much a part of the community as you are. Take your local street person out for a coffee or a meal. Get talking to them. It'll give you a new perspective.

5. Say "Good Morning" to your local police officer. They are patrolling your neighbourhood for your safety. Ask them about how the war on crime is going, or whether they have come across a good murder recently.

6. Shovel the snow or brush the leaves or cut the hedge outside your own house. But also do this for a stranger's front garden . . . just for the heck of it . . . without being asked and without needing to be thanked.

COMMON GROUND PROMOTES LOCAL DISTINCTIVENESS

www.commonground.org.uk

7. Donate your old books and unwanted presents to your local charity shop. Or sell them on eBay and donate the proceeds.

8. Go to your next town council meeting. Get to know your local councillors. Take part in the politics of your local community.

9. Join a neighbourhood association. There will be lots of local societies organizing all sort of things in your area. Find out about who's doing what. Join. Participate actively. Volunteer.

10. Organize a block party. Or a quiz evening. Or an outdoor concert. Create an outbreak of festivity. Break down the barriers between young and old, rich and poor, the long-established and the newcomers. Have a lot of fun.

*Guerrilla gardening...

. . . means planting flowers on vacant land. It might be around the base of a tree, or along the side of a foot-path, or even in the cracks of paving stones. All you need are the seeds, a bag of soil, a trowel and a watering can. For more information, visit one of these websites:

Primal Seeds:
www.primalseeds.org/guerrilla.htm

Guerrilla Gardening:
www.guerrillagardening.org

GO ON HOLIDAY... AND CHANGE THE WORLD

There are lots of ways of changing the world whilst you are on holiday.

- **You can do practical conservation or development work as a volunteer** – from a short conservation holiday to a longer volunteer placement. For world-wide volunteering opportunities, check out: www.worldwidevolunteering.org.uk

- **You can give online,** and then arrange to visit the project or person you have supported.

- **You can visit local projects** – from prisons to homes for handicapped kids, from tribal tea plantations to women's cooperatives and street children's banks. These may all be much more interesting than another day of museums and temples. Just ask around when you arrive. Somebody where you are staying will be able to suggest some great projects to visit.

If you decide to travel by air, think about the climate change impact. There are lots of websites where you can offset your CO_2 emissions.

www.wwoof.org

Spend a working holiday on an organic farm

First it was:
Working Weekends On Organic Farms

Then it became:
Willing Workers On Organic Farms

Now it's known as:
World-Wide Opportunities On Organic Farms

WWOOF was started in England in 1971 when Sue Coppard, a London secretary, wanted to provide opportunities for people like herself to spend time in the countryside supporting the organic movement, making new friends and sharing ideas on sustainable living.

Sue's first working weekend involved four people and took place at Emerson College, a biodynamic farm run by the Rudolf Steiner movement in Sussex. The weekend was a great success. People heard about it. Demand started to grow. Sue found that many organic farmers and smallholders were keen to have WWOOFers come and work for them on this basis.

You can now WWOOF all over the world and for longer than a weekend. WWOOFers work in exchange for food and accommodation. The farms come in all shapes and sizes: large manor houses to smallholdings, and everything in between, which are either growing organically or in the process of converting.

WWOOFing is a wonderful way to contribute to the health of the planet and to attend to your own health at the same time.

...OR SET UP YOUR OWN AID AGENCY

Marc Gold did just that. He had dreamed about going to India since he was seven. In 1989, thirty-three years later, he actually went. Whilst there, he met a Tibetan woman in the Himalayas who had terrible ear infections. He was able to save her life by buying her antibiotics costing $1. And another $30 provided her with a hearing aid. He was amazed to see that he could do so much with so little.

After he got back, he set up his 100 Friends project. It was a really simple idea. Before going on his next trip, he would send a letter to 100 people asking for support. For his next trip, which was in 1992 and again to India, he expected to raise $400. To his surprise, his 100 friends contributed more than $2,200 – which goes a long way in India.

Since then he has raised money nearly every year to take to a Third World country. He travels there at his own expense, and tries to find ways of putting the money to work "in the most compassionate, appropriate, culturally compatible, constructive and practical manner possible". He tries to find people in need who are not being helped by anyone else.

Marc has now completed fifteen trips and distributed over $180,000. His goal is to raise

and then donate at least $1 million. In 2007-08 he built two schools, one in Afghanistan and one in Cambodia. He has been to Afghanistan, Bangladesh, Cambodia, China, India, Indonesia, Laos, Mozambique, Myanmar, Nepal, Pakistan, Palestine, Philippines, South Africa, Sri Lanka, Sudan, Thailand, Tibet, Turkey and Vietnam.

Nearly 90 per cent of the funds are given directly to individuals (especially women and children) and to grassroots organizations. This is a far higher proportion than established agencies such as Oxfam or Save the Children can achieve. The money is used for medical costs, education, vocational training and setting people up in business, emergency aid and other purposes.

Marc often suggests that part of the grant is given to someone else. "For example, if I give 1,500 Rupees (approximately $33), I might suggest that the recipient gives something like 100 Rupees to someone else who is even more needy. People seem to brighten when I suggest this, perhaps because it makes them feel part of a larger cycle of giving and receiving."

You don't have to be Oxfam or Save the Children to do something about Third World poverty. Become one of Marc's 100 Friends, or be inspired by what he has done and do the same yourself: www.100friends.com

Pass on your ideas for places to visit and things to see

Wikitravel is like the Wikipedia encyclopaedia, but for travellers. Wikitravel is written by travellers for travellers. Anyone can contribute an article or add a recommendation – including you. Started in 2003, there are now 12,000 articles so far. **http://wikitravel.org**

www.100friends.com

15

MORE THINGS TO DO:

40

Here are fifteen more ideas for the everyday activist. All are simple and fun to do.

1. Get a dot.tv web address.

Dot.tv is a Tuvalu registration, and a royalty goes to the government of this tiny island country in the South Pacific. Tuvalu is the second most threatened country in the world. Its six islands are about to be overwhelmed by the rising ocean level. Get yourself a funky web address and find out about the problems of global warming. **www.tv**

2. Stop doing Su-Do-Ku.

Spend your time doing something more useful – like changing the world. Half an hour a day equals 183 hours a year; that's nearly eight days out of a year for doing something more useful.

3. SUV off.

Sport utility vehicles or 4x4s consume huge quantities of fuel and clog up the streets. Hummers are even worse. Download fake parking tickets from the Wastemonsters site and put them under the windscreen wipers. These tickets give information on why people should *not* drive these cars. **www.stopurban4x4s.org.uk**

4. Plant one tree.

It could be your birth tree. Or why not a beech tree which emits sufficient oxygen for a family of four. Get yourself an ice cream container and some soil; plant a seed. Watch it grow. When it's ready plant it out in your garden, in a wood, by the side of a road ... somewhere where a tree's needed. Find out about your birth tree: **www.geocities.com/athens/5341/tree.html**

5. Cross your books.

Find a book you have read and really liked. Register it on the Bookcrossing website. Write a note telling anyone who finds it what to do (the instructions are on the website). And leave it for someone to pick up. Your book has become part of the world's biggest free library. **www.bookcrossing.com**

6. Make open source cola.

This is a recipe which has been perfected by consumers – just as Linux software was developed by its users. Understand the principles of "open source" and "copyleft" and that profit is not the only mechanism for getting things done. Have yourself a cola party to celebrate your new global brand. **www.colawp.com/colas/400/cola467_recipe.html**

7. Commit a random act of kindness today. Think up something wonderful and unexpected. Leave a note telling them that it

was a random act of kindness, and perhaps they might like to do something themselves for someone else.

8. Go nuclear trainspotting.

Track the trains as they carry nuclear fuels and nuclear waste around the country. If people know more about the potential dangers, they may ask harder questions when it comes to building more nuclear power stations. **www.fnord.demon.co.uk/mt/third/nukemap.html**

9. Get a RED credit card.

Product RED raises money for the Global Fund to fight the world's three killer diseases: AIDS, TB and malaria. Use the American Express RED card, there is no annual fee. £5 if you use the card in the first month and 1 per cent of your spending are given to the Global Fund (1.25 per cent if you spend more than £5,000 in a year). **www.joinred.com**

10. Keep the beaches clean (if you live by the sea).

If you find any foreign garbage on your beach, contact Global Garbage, a Brazilian initiative which tracks and displays long-distance garbage found littering beaches. It's amazing how far litter can travel. www.globalgarbage.org And find out more about its impact. **www.marine-litter.gpa.unep.org**

11. Mark your banknotes.

Make your money talk. Put a simple slogan or the URL of a website. The banknote will pass through many hands during the course of its life.

12. Join a Freecycling group.

Find new owners for things you no longer need. It might be just what somebody else is looking for. At the same time, find the things that you need or want: **www.freecycle.org**

13. Go cycling in the buff.

The bicycle is the most energy efficient means of transport, and in gridlocked cities, it can even be the quickest. Go as a bare as you dare on the next World Naked Bike Ride: www.worldnakedbikeride.org. Or join a Critical Mass where cyclists come together to assert their presence by cycling slowly round the city centre: **www.critical-mass.org**

14. Save a disappearing language.

A lost language means a loss of cultural diversity. All you need to do is to choose an endangered language and learn it. Learn Chinook or Cornish at **www.word2word.com/course.html**

15. Get a second life.

Join this fantasy website. Create an avatar, decide your character, your look, your personality. Become a campaigner for justice or a fundraiser for charity in this online world. Raise Linden Dollars for the cause, then convert to real money: **http://secondlife.com**

THERE ARE LOTS MORE IDEAS WHERE THESE CAME FROM. READ 365 WAYS TO CHANGE THE WORLD OR GO TO

www.365act.com

ONE THING CAN LEAD TO ANOTHER

Start doing something quite simple – by yourself or with others.

Enjoy yourself. Recognize that you are doing something to change the world, even if it's only quite small. The sense of having done something will then inspire you to do more. For example...

1. You start by clicking on the rainforest site, and your click actually buys one square metre of rainforest. Try doing this at: **www.therainforestsite.com**

2. You realize that you can do this once a day. So you make the Rainforest Site the Home Page on your web browser. Each morning when you open up your computer, the Rainforest Site appears and invites you to click to save another square metre. You do this. You're now saving the rainforest at the rate of 365 square metres a year.

3. You tell 11 of your friends. They all get excited by the idea. So you set up the Southgate Clickers – you all live in Southgate. Everyone clicks once a day. Together you are now saving over 4,000 square metres of rainforest a year – that's about the size of a football pitch. All your clicks actually release money from the site's sponsor to buy all these square metres. You're lucky that the land isn't as expensive as downtown Chicago or Lisbon!

4. The Southgate Clickers decide to meet once a month for a cup of coffee and – because you are now beginning to get interested – to see what more you can do to save the rainforest. Some of the group decide to go to the Amazon for their next holiday and visit all the trees they have saved. Of course, you plant some more trees to offset the carbon emissions of your flight.

5. You are stunned by how big the rainforest is and the urgent need to protect as much of it as possible. So you agree you will all do much more when you get back. You decide to recruit eighty-eight more clickers, and to ask each clicker to host one fundraising dinner in their home each year, where all the guests are asked to contribute £10 each to your Rainforest Fund.

6. You're beginning to raise serious money – around £10,000 a year. So you decide to set up the Amazon Foundation. Someone comes up with a great idea for a possible sponsor!

7. Another clicker draws your attention to the National Lottery's international grants fund. You submit a project proposal to provide sustainable livelihoods for indigenous forest dwellers working with one of the organizations you visited on your holiday. You're becoming a real NGO now.

8. Someone else draws your attention to the Sloth Club. You're intrigued by the fact that members have to try to "live like a sloth". So you decide to join.

9. You want to find out more. You start researching the whole issue of the rainforest and its importance to the planet's health. You become well informed on the subject. You write letters to politicians urging them to do something, and to the newspapers urging the public to join your Rainforest Campaign.

10. On your next visit to the Amazon, you fall in love with the scenery and even learn to like beans and rice. You decide to stay on. You sell your home and use the money to set up a camp for foreign visitors to learn about the rainforest and undertake practical conservation work.

This all started with one click. By stages you got intrigued, then involved, then passionate. You decided to join the "Great Escape" from your polluted and congested city, and to "downsize" your job and your life to something you felt happier doing. You ended up a rainforest expert and activist.

Or maybe you just kept your 9 to 5 job as a shop assistant or a bank clerk, hoping for promotion and a pay rise, but also happily doing your one click a day to save the rainforest.

Get started today. You never know how things might turn out!

The Sloth Club

Anja Light, Australian singer and rainforest activist, and members of the Japanese Action for Mangrove Reforestation were in the coastal jungle of Ecuador. As they were passing through a village, they saw a sloth tied up in a concrete cage in a kitchen, waiting to be ordered as somebody's dinner. Something about its sheer defencelessness moved them. They bought it for five dollars and released it downriver into a forest reserve. An hour later the group reached the next town, where they saw another sloth for sale. They realized that it was impossible to buy up all the sloths. So the idea of the Sloth Club was born to raise money to protect and restore forests and improve the lives of forest communities . . . and to lead a cultural movement promoting values inspired by the sloth's low-energy and non-violent habits.

www.slothclub.org

Chapter 3
What's the problem?

Now you're beginning to get into the swing of things. The next step is to identify the problems that are really important to *you* – in your life, in your community, in your country, in the wider world. What do you want to see made better? And are you prepared to do something about it?

WHAT'S WRONG WITH YOUR WORLD?

The world is a big place, and there are lots of problems. You can't solve them all. If you want to make a real impact, you need to think a little about where you are going to focus your efforts. These are some of the issues you might be interested in:

... the way you live your life

Where to start... not enough exercise, drive everywhere, have a mountain of credit card debts, seldom smile, don't volunteer or give to charity...

... at home and with your family

We're real eco-sinners... eat junk food, watch too much TV, don't recycle enough, waste too much energy...

... your neighbourhood

There are lots of problems... graffiti and street litter, too few trees, the traffic menace and road accidents, a failing school, not enough green space and no swimming pools...

... your city

Congestion and sometimes gridlock, poor and too expensive public transport, they're planning to knock everything down for a senseless redevelopment, homelessness, rising street crime...

... at work

I'm stressed out and bored, the company's not very socially responsible, why are we not drinking Fairtrade tea and coffee?, I'm sure there's sexism at the workplace...

... your ethnicity or religion

It's all so confusing... misunderstanding and stereotyping, racism and discrimination, conflicts between traditional and modern values...

... your country

Our politicians are windbags and nobody bothers to vote; they lied to us over weapons of mass destruction and look at the consequences; the drug laws are senseless;, we don't want nuclear power...

... the big wide world

It's full of problems... poverty and inequality, AIDS, TB and malaria, conflict, corruption and bad governance, hunger, lack of access to water and poor sanitation, warfare, the arms trade, refugees, torture and abuse of human rights...

... the planet

The oceans are polluted and now almost fish-free, species and rainforest are vanishing at an alarming rate, global warming is changing everything...

... cyberspace

Too much spam (I really don't need Viagra), child pornography, the spirit of the Web is being lost and it's all becoming far too commercial...

...and even out there in space

Satellites that invade our privacy, star wars and the militarization of space, our failure to find extraterrestrials...

A GOOD STARTING POINT IS *YOU*

Ask yourself these four questions:

1. What is wrong where you live and work?

2. What are the issues that really concern you?

3. What are you interested in?

4. What do you passionately believe in?

Use the answers to help you decide what it is you want to do.

TRIGGER POINTS

Saul of Tarsus (better known now as St Paul)

had set out from Jerusalem for Damascus in the year AD 36. He had a letter from the High Priest authorizing him to arrest any followers of Jesus whom he could find in Damascus. *. . . and as he journeyed, he came near Damascus: and suddenly there shined round about him a light from heaven. And he fell to the earth, and heard a voice saying unto him, Saul, Saul, why persecutest thou me?* (Acts of the Apostles, 9:3-4)

This blinding flash of light was the "trigger point" which changed Paul from a persecutor of Christians to an evangelist who would go out and lay the foundations for Christianity as a world religion.

Many people will have their own trigger point where they suddenly become aware of the importance of an issue and are motivated to do something about it. Your trigger point may not be as dramatic as Paul's, but it could be equally effective in changing you from a passive observer to an active change-maker. It could even change the course of your life.

These are some ways that your interest in an issue could be triggered:

• You meet a person or hear them speak; what they have to say inspires you.

• You come across an idea for the first time, and this catches your imagination.

• You or someone close to you has an experience which means that nothing will ever be quite the same again.

• You read some compelling facts which give you a completely new perspective about an issue and its importance.

• You see a programme on TV or read a book or visit a website, and suddenly everything becomes clear to you.

So what's your trigger point? What's going to inspire you to take action?

How to be inspired

If you are looking for inspiration, here are a few things you might do:

• Get out and about; meet lots of people. You will find that some of them will be interesting, and if you are lucky, one or two will be inspirational.

• Go to meetings, and get to talk to the speakers and discuss your ideas with them. Don't be shy!

• Read books about the world and its problems. For example, if you read *When the rivers run dry* by Fred Pearce, you will probably become a water activist. If you read *High Tide* by Mark Lynas, you'll realize that something really does need to be done about global warming. Or take a look at *WorldChanging*, a compendium of problems and solutions: **www.worldchanging.org**

• Visit projects where people are trying to do something positive. Look at the problems they are tackling, see their successes, discuss the issues with them.

• If there's an issue you feel really strongly about, think whether there is one person you would really like to meet, whose views you admire and whose advice you would respect. Then find a way of getting to meet them.

• Go to the next World Social Forum, which is held annually in January to show that "another world is possible" where you will meet activists from all over the world. Find out where the next one will be held at **www.forumsocialmundial.org.br**

If you've got a few moments to spare, then do these things:

- Visit the Right Livelihood Awards website and "meet" some of the award winners. Four people are honoured each year for their contribution to a better world and to social justice. **www.rightlivelihood.org**

- Check out some of the Ashoka fellows. They are leading social entrepreneurs from around the world who are offered bursaries to help them develop their ideas further. **www.ashoka.org**

- Listen to the BBC World Service online. It broadcasts some excellent programmes covering many of the issues facing the future of the planet. **www.bbc.co.uk/worldservice**

Right Livelihood Awards

The Right Livelihood Awards, founded in 1980, are often referred to as the "Alternative Nobel Prizes". They were introduced "to honour and support those offering practical and exemplary answers to the most urgent challenges facing us today". The initial funding was provided by Jakob von Uexkull, a Swedish-German professional philatelist, with the proceeds from the sale of his business. Since then, the Awards have been supported by individual donors. The annual prize money is $275,000.

The 2006 awards were shared by:

- **Daniel Ellsberg** (USA), whose whistleblowing helped end the Vietnam War, was awarded *"for putting peace and truth first, at considerable personal risk, and dedicating his life to inspiring others to follow his example"*.

- **Ruth Manorama** (India), organizer of and advocate for Dalit women, belonging to the scheduled castes (sometimes also called "untouchables"). Manorama, a Dalit herself, was honoured *"for her commitment over decades to achieving equality for Dalit women, building effective and committed women's organizations and working for their rights at national and international levels"*.

- **The Festival Internacional de Poesia de Medellin** (Colombia), a poetry festival which has helped build peace in one of the most violent cities in the world, showed *"how creativity, beauty, free expression and community can flourish amongst and overcome even deeply entrenched fear and violence"*.

The 2006 Honorary Award went to **Chico Whitaker Ferreira** (Brazil) *"for a lifetime's dedicated work for social justice that has strengthened democracy in Brazil and helped give birth to the World Social Forum"*.

49

TEST YOURSELF...

Take one of these tests. Learn a bit more about yourself and the impact of your lifestyle. It may even spur you into action.

Are you a racist?

Take a Project Implicit test to measure your attitudes. Are you a racist, an ageist, a sexist, a homophobe? Find out. **https://implicit.harvard.edu/implicit**

How big is your ecological footprint?

An ecological footprint is the amount of land and water area a person needs to provide the resources consumed and to absorb the waste produced, using prevailing technology. Footprinting is used as an indicator of environmental sustainability. Measure your footprint at: **www.bestfootforward.com/footprintlife.htm www.bestfootforward.com/ecocal.htm**

Measure your CO_2 emissions

You directly cause CO_2 to be produced from the energy used at home and from your transport. You indirectly cause CO_2 to be produced through all the goods and services you consume. To reduce global warming requires people to reduce their CO_2 emissions. Calculate yours, and find out how to reduce them: **www.carboncalculator.com** and make a pledge to reduce at **www.lickglobalwarming.com**

...OR PLAY THE GAME

Run a Banana Republic

Do you have what it takes to be a Dictator? Find out. Play Banana Republic. You will need two to five other people to play this game with you. Your goal is to become President of your country. Then you have to remain President for long enough to collect enough medals and become President-for-Life. If you understand the issues, you will be better equipped to fight corruption. Get Banana Republic from: **www.benco-boardgames.com/bananarepublic-game.htm**

Be a Peace Maker

PeaceMaker is a one-player game in which the player can choose to take the role of either the Israeli Prime Minister or the Palestinian President. The player must react to in-game events, from diplomatic negotiations to military attacks, and interact with eight other political leaders and social groups in order to establish a stable resolution to the conflict before his or her term in office ends. **www.peacemakergame.com**

Live in a refugee camp

In Darfur in Western Sudan, genocide is occurring. Each day civilians face the possibility of mass killing, torture, rape, having their village burnt to the ground, theft of all their property and severe human rights abuse. Find out what life is like. Play Darfur is Dying. **www.darfurisdying.com**

Deliver food to the hungry

A major crisis has developed on the island of Sheylan in the Indian Ocean. A new team is being sent to enhance the World Food Programme's presence and help feed millions of hungry people. Your job is to provide food aid. Play Food Force. **www.food-force.com**

EXPERIENCING THE PROBLEM

Your own personal experiences can provide you with a starting point.

For example, Suzy Lamplugh, an estate agent, went to meet a "Mr Kipper" to show him a property, but she never returned. Suzy's mother, Diana, decided to devote the rest of her life to the issue of personal safety. She founded the Suzy Lamplugh Trust in Suzy's memory to promote this cause.

A child contracting diabetes or being killed in a road accident . . . a long wait at Accident & Emergency in the most unpleasant room without any facilities for whiling away the time or getting a glass of water . . . graffiti disfiguring a brick wall . . . each day you will find lots of things that concern or even outrage you enough to want to do something.

Water carrying

It was a cool, sunny early morning in eastern Uganda. I decided to go for a walk. As I was scrambling around the side of a mountain, I saw an old woman carrying a headload of firewood that seemed unbelievably heavy. I thought about offering to help, but realized that there was no way that I, a healthy adult male, could walk with such a weight on my head. Next I passed a group of women and girls carrying water back from the stream balancing large tin cans on their head . . .

Now imagine waking up long before sunrise and then walking for an hour or more to the nearest river, and then carrying a bucket full of water on your head all the way home. As a woman or a young girl, it is your responsibility to do this every day of your life!

This is a reality for millions around the world who don't have water on tap. With the water so hard to get, there's very little to use. What quality of life could you expect from one bucket for your whole family? How could you wash, drink, clean, cook or even grow vegetables? How much time and energy does it take to provide your family with this most basic human requirement?

If you had to do it, would you put up with it? Or would you search for a solution?

In South Africa, Louis Groenewald certainly thought that things could be done differently. His Hippo Water Roller allows women to fetch four times the amount of water by rolling it home from the dam or stream. In India, Anil Gupta and his colleagues at the Honeybee Network also thought so. They designed a Water Jacket for Rajasthani women to carry their water, which spread the weight across their whole body.

Creating simple solutions to the everyday problems of the world's poor can do far more than throwing buckets of aid at the problem. We should use our brains as well as our bank accounts to change the world.

www.hipporoller.org
www.sristi.org/honeybee.html

51

Eat in the dark

If you want to understand the problems that disabled people face in living their lives, the best way is to experience the problems at first hand. You might try using a wheelchair for a day. You would get really cross at the kerbs, steps and stairs that were making it hard or impossible for you to get around the city. For the first time you would really understand the importance of wheelchair accessibility.

But why not try eating in the dark to find out what it's like being blind? This is the brainchild of two Frenchmen, Edouard de Broglie and Etienne Boisrond. They set up a restaurant called Dans le Noir? in Paris, where diners dine in complete darkness, and where the waiters are blind. They felt that the darkness would heighten the senses of taste and smell. But what the experience really does is show how disabled we are in the complete dark (even watches have to be taken off because of their luminous glow), and the ability that blind people have developed to cope in this environment.

Try finding and eating the last few peas on your plate (don't cheat by using your fingers) or pouring a glass of wine in the complete dark. It will make you much more sensitive to the issues of blindness and disability.

Dans le Noir? has now opened in London. They also organize "in the dark" special events. There are other blind restaurants in Switzerland, Germany and Finland.

www.danslenoir.com

www.unsicht-bar.com

www.blinde-kuh.de

Take a toxic tour

Your neighbourhood may be well cared for and look great, but underneath the surface you will find a mass of waste.

- Human waste that goes into the sewers.
- Household waste that goes for recycling or into a landfill. This includes all the cartons and packaging that comes with what we buy.
- Furniture and equipment that we no longer need or which has broken down.

All this waste needs to be disposed of.

Find out more about the waste we create. Go on a toxic tour. Visit a recycling centre or a landfill site or a sewage treatment plant.

A CHANCE MEETING

53

"Summer 2004: I was at university. That morning, I woke up in good spirits. Not many students were around, as most had gone home for the holidays.

"As I was walking along a footpath, a few metres ahead I saw a young boy. He looked unbelievably sad. I was so concerned that I asked him what his problem was. He told me that he had lost his bread, which was what he was going to eat for his dinner, and that he didn't know what to do.

"The problem was insignificant to me, but really serious for him. I knew I could sort it out very easily. So I did. I took the boy to a shop and bought him all the food he needed.

"As we walked together, he confided to me. I learned that he was an orphan from Vietnam, who had recently come to the UK. His parents had been killed, which he found hard to talk about. I believe he was in some form of refugee resettlement programme. But I did not discover how he had arrived in the UK, or who was taking care of him. A friend later told me that

he had been sleeping in empty student rooms on the university campus.

"When it was time for us to part, he hugged me goodbye. I would have liked to have spoken to him again. But he did not reappear. I hoped that this was because he had been fostered or adopted.

"Meeting this boy was a significant turning point in my life. I was happy to have been able to help him. But I realised that a great more could be done for people suffering poverty, distress and injustice."

Nkem Nwachukwu is a twenty-four-year-old Nigerian now living in London. After a degree in Politics and International Relations, she worked as an intern at the African, Caribbean and Pacific States Secretariat in Brussels. She organizes Performance Nights to raise money for "Seeds for Africa" which helps needy African families by providing them with indigenous vegetable seeds, agricultural equipment and technical advice.

www.seedsforafrica.org

BEING THERE

Some people live through extraordinary situations – perhaps a war, a famine or a tsunami – which provides them with a life-changing experience and the opportunity to do something creative for a better world. Others make a decision to go to where the action is and get involved. Tim Clancy was one such person.

Tim left university in 1992. Travelling and working in Europe that summer brought him into contact with people actively opposing the growing conflict in the former Yugoslavia. He decided to go there.

Within a few days of arriving in Zagreb (in Croatia), he had volunteered with a local relief agency, Suncokret, to work in refugee camps first in Herzegovina, and then in Bosnia and Croatia. He was in Mostar during the siege and destruction, worked on reconstruction and development in the years following, and during the 1999 Kosovo crisis, worked with Save the Children to establish safe zones for children in Albania and Kosovo.

After the conflict had ended, he made Sarajevo his home and spent a year trekking in Bosnia to find out more about highland culture and living conditions.

In 2000, he co-founded Green Visions to promote environmental conservation and sustainable tourism. In 2004, he founded Earth in Mind as a forum for those who believe a better world is possible, and also wrote the first tourist guide to Bosnia and Herzegovina.

Find somewhere interesting to go. Let your journey begin.

Some places to go to:

• **Rwanda**, to see the aftermath of the genocide and what's being done to build bridges between Hutus and Tutsis.

• **Darfur,** which is where the most recent genocide is happening right now, despite all our pledges of "Never again".

• **Tuvalu,** to see an island nation sinking into the sea as a result of global warming.

• **Siberia and Alaska,** to see the permafrost melting for the same reason.

• **Gaza,** the most crowded territory on earth and the epicentre of Middle East unrest, now complicated by fractured relationships between Hamas and Fatah.

• **Israel,** to get the other perspective, and to find projects where Israeli Jews and Arabs are working together for peace.

• **Nagapattanam** in south India, to see communities being rebuilt after the tsunami.

- **Sierra Leone,** the world's poorest nation, to see how the pieces are being picked up after decades of war.

- **Cape Town and Cape Flats** in South Africa, to visit the city with the greatest division between rich and poor.

- **Lagos** in Nigeria, to experience life in one of the world's great oil-producing nations.

- **North Korea,** part of Bush's "Axis of Evil" where you might be the only tourist.

- **Iraq,** to make up your own mind as to whether the overthrow of Saddam Hussein was a good thing or not.

- **Shanghai,** the commercial centre of the new China, a city with an astronomical economic growth rate.

- **Bolivia,** to get a take on the new left politics sweeping some of the countries in South America.

Find out about the world from a different perspective

Many information sources are located in the North and see the world from a Northern perspective. Here are three websites which will give a more "Southern" view of the world and its problems:

Indymedia: an anti-globalization news network. http://www.indymedia.org, with another website for radio programmes: http://radio.indymedia.org

Inter-Press Service: a public-benefit organization for development cooperation disseminating information with particular regard to the developing countries. IPS publishes a number of e-newsletters. www.ips.org/newsletters.shtml

Third World Network: information and publications that look at development issues from a Southern perspective. www.twnside.org.sg

KILLER FACTS

Sometimes you come across a fact which is so powerful that it changes your whole outlook. Try some of these on for size:

Some killer facts about clean water

Two billion people lack access to clean water and sanitation. More than 22 million people die each year, mostly children, from diseases associated with poor water and sanitary conditions.

About 90 per cent of sewage and 70 per cent of industrial waste in developing countries are discharged without treatment, often polluting the usable water supply.

Millennium Development Goal 7 aims to reduce by half the number of people in the world without access to clean drinking water.

UNICEF reckons that meeting the MDG targets on water and sanitation would cost an additional $11.3 billion each year.

The global bottled water industry is now worth $22 billion a year.

Does it sound obscene that whilst we are consuming the latest "designer water", billions are struggling to get their daily water needs which are often polluted or barely drinkable? What are you going to do about it?

You could, for example:

• Ask for a glass of tap water with a slice of lemon whenever you eat out in a restaurant.

• Empathize with the difficulties that people are facing by using some of the low-tech solutions that are available. Try collecting dirty water, purifying it and then drinking it using the SODIS system, which uses sunlight to make it drinkable.

• Join the Young Water Action Team, a network of young people doing something about the water problem worldwide.

SODIS: **www.sodis.ch**

Young Water Action Team: **www.ywat.org**

See what Reed Paget and the pupils at Fyndoune Community College are doing about the water issue *(see page 80)*.

Some killer facts about cotton

Cotton consumes 22 per cent of the world's pesticides, though it is planted on only 3 per cent of the world's fields. One T-shirt needs one cupful of fertilizer and pesticide.

By weight 30 per cent of a cotton garment is chemical residue; what we put next to our skin is easily absorbed by the body.

Cotton grows best in a hot dry climate, but requires a lot of water. The cotton needed to make just one T-shirt requires 1,170 litres of water – that's more than a tonne. In countries such as Egypt, Pakistan and the central Asian republics of Uzbekistan, Tajikistan and

Turkmenistan, cotton is a major export crop and growing it is leading to serious water and environmental problems. The Aral Sea has shrunk and is in danger of disappearing altogether. The once-mighty Indus has become a trickle, and the intensively irrigated fields are becoming salty which will lead to desertification of the land. All of this due in large part to cotton growing.

Why not switch to hemp? Hemp grows well in cooler climates where it grows easily and quickly (in just 120 days), smothers weeds and needs little or no irrigation. Hemp is a bit coarse to wear on its own. But if you buy a hemp-cotton mix T-shirt, you will more than halve the water footprint of your purchase.

It's an unfair world

- 18 million people a year or 50,000 per day die as a result of poverty.
- Every year nearly 11 million children die before their fifth birthday.
- 800 million people go to bed hungry each night.
- The three richest people in the world control more wealth than all 600 million people living in the world's poorest countries.

The Solution

Eradication of extreme poverty and hunger in the world by 2015 is a Millennium Development Goal. The Sachs Report proposed some "quick wins", which would make a positive impact at relatively modest cost:

- Eliminate school fees.
- Provide free school meals.
- Provide soil nutrients to farmers in sub-Saharan Africa.
- Promote breast-feeding.
- Deworm school children (in affected areas).
- End user fees for basic health care.
- Provide community health training in rural areas.
- Provide information on sexual and reproductive health.
- Provide mosquito nets.
- Provide drugs for AIDS, tuberculosis, and malaria.
- Upgrade slums.
- Make land available for public housing.
- Provide access to electricity, water and sanitation.
- Plant trees.
- Legislate for women's rights, including property rights.
- Take action against domestic violence.
- Appoint government scientific advisors in each country.

FACTS THAT SHOULD CHANGE THE WORLD

58

Jessica Williams wrote a best-selling book called *50 facts that should change the world* (2004). Note the use of the word *should*, rather than *will*. It is not the facts that will change the world, but whether people respond to the facts . . . and what they then do about it.

Are there facts that will make you want to change the world?

If you are already committed to doing something, what facts can you find which will make a compelling case and encourage others to join with you?

These are some "killer facts" from Jessica's book and from other sources:

Every cow in the European Union is subsidized by $2.20 a day; that's more than what 75 per cent of Africans have to live on . . . and their belching creates a serious methane problem. Will this provoke you to campaign for fairer trade or do something about world poverty?

A kiwi fruit flown from New Zealand to the UK causes five times its weight in greenhouse gases to be emitted. Will this make you think of ways of reducing your food miles by giving up kiwis or buying local?

Cars kill two people every minute of every day of every year . . . and injure or cripple another seventeen. Around 40,000 people will die on the roads of the USA this year. On 9/11, the total number of people who died at the World Trade Center, the Pentagon and aboard the four aircraft was 2,976. Does this make you want to campaign for a much more serious response by governments to the global epidemic of road deaths?

More people die each year from suicide than in all the world's armed conflicts. In the USA in 2000, there were 1.7 times more homicides than suicides. In Britain, a study in 2002 showed that nearly one in six adults had considered attempting suicide. Should we be finding ways of spreading happiness or be campaigning for better mental health services?

FINDING OUT THE FACTS

It's never been easier to find the facts. No longer do you have to climb up to the attic to consult a huge encyclopedia which is probably out of date. You can find out all you need to know almost instantly by searching on the Internet. Here are some sources:

- Put your key words into Google and see what it comes up with.

- Search the Wikipedia. This is an Internet encyclopedia compiled by the users. If there's nothing about the subject you are interested in, create a new entry. If you have important information to add to an existing entry, add to the entry: **http://en.wikipedia.org**

- Search the Open Directory. This is a directory of websites, and like the Wikipedia is constructed and maintained by a vast, global community of volunteer editors:
http://dmoz.org

- Go to the website of an organization that you've heard about, and follow the links through to other organizations. You never know where you might end up.

- Get hold of a copy of *The State of the World Atlas* and companion volumes on war, women, water, health and food which display comparative information from around the world using maps; produced by Myriad Editions: **www.myriadeditions.com**

- The Princeton website has Infographic posters on themes such as weapons, water, transport, smoking and Starbucks and McDonald's plus ready-to-use Powerpoint presentations on a range of social issues:
www.princeton.edu/%7eina/ infographics/index.html

www.princeton.edu/%7eina/thematic_ presentations/index.html

- Worldmapper has data on a wide range of social issues, where the size of a country on the map is made proportional to its contribution to the theme being mapped. Nearly 200 maps cover issues as diverse as rainfall, migration, nuclear power and wealth.
www.worldmapper.org

Do this:

Take one of the following subjects and discover ten interesting facts about it:

Inequality and poverty in the world

Gender inequality in your country or in the world

The arms trade

Global warming

Best of all, take the issue that particularly concerns you.

I HAVE
A DREAM

The process of changing the world will often start with a dream of how things might be. Your job then is simply to make your dream come true.

Nkosi's dream

Nkosi Xolani Johnson, born on 4 February 1989, was South Africa's longest surviving child born HIV-positive. In July 2000, he addressed the 13th International AIDS Conference in Durban, and the speech which he wrote himself was televised worldwide. This did much to highlight the importance of the AIDS issue in his own country and to bring attention to children born with the virus. Nkosi died on 1 June 2001. Here are some extracts from Nkosi's speech:

"Hi! My name is Nkosi Johnson. I live in Melville, Johannesburg, South Africa. I am eleven years old, and I have full-blown AIDS. I was born HIV-positive.

"When I was two years old, I was living in a care centre for HIV/AIDS-infected people. My mommy . . . could not afford to keep me because she was very scared that the community. . . would find out that we were both infected and chase us away. I know she loved me very much . . . Then the care centre had to close down because they did not have any funds. Gail Johnson [a Director of the centre] . . . said that she would take me home . . . I have been living with her for eight years now.

"I know that my blood is only dangerous to other people if they also have an open wound and my blood goes into it. That is the only time that people need to be careful when touching me . . . Care for us and accept us. We are all human beings. We are normal. We have hands. We have feet. We can walk. We can talk. We have needs just like everyone else. Don't be afraid of us. We are all the same . . .

"Because I was separated from my mother at an early age, my Mommy Gail and I have always wanted to start a care centre for HIV/AIDS mothers and their children. I am very happy and proud to say that the first Nkosi's Haven opened last year, and we look after ten mommies and fifteen children. My Mommy Gail and I want to open five Nkosi's Havens by the end of next year, because I want more infected mothers to stay together with their children."

This was Nkosi's dream. What's yours?

NKOSI JOHNSON AIDS FOUNDATION:

www.nkosi.iafrica.com

42 million people worldwide are living with HIV/AIDS today, and 5 million became newly infected in 2002.

25 million children will have been orphaned as a result of AIDS by the year 2010. Every fourteen seconds another child becomes an AIDS orphan.

55 per cent of the HIV/AIDS infected population in Africa are girls and women. Because of culture, attitudes to sex, poverty and lack of education, females are infected with hiv more often than men.

GWEN'S DREAM

Gwen Rolfe was eleven years old when her teacher asked her to write about her vision for a better world. Gwen's idea was for a community where everyone worked together and supported each other, a place where people invested their own time for the good of where they lived. The whole community would become a better place for everyone. The teacher ridiculed Gwen's idea as being unsustainable because people wouldn't give up their time and energy and possibly their money without getting something in return.

Gwen felt humiliated. She felt that her ideas were worthless and that nobody would ever want to listen to her. She left school early, and set about becoming a mother. She had four children by the time she was twenty-four.

It was around ten years later that Gwen came across the *School for Social Entrepreneurs*. They were looking for five people in Salford with ideas and energy whom they would help start projects to improve the health of local people. Salford is the twin city of Manchester where in 1844 Friedrich Engels wrote his celebrated book *The Condition of the Working Class in England*. Gwen suddenly remembered all her teenage dreams and enthusiasms, plucked up her courage and decided to enrol.

During the year of the programme, Gwen started the Tinytots Vision community nursery in Salford, to help other young mothers by providing childcare and jobs for local people, and then investing the profits back into the community. This was the same vision that her teacher had squashed.

She did it. Eight years later, the project is thriving. Gwen has raised nearly £1 million in grants to make it happen. *"It really is a dream come true, and it is totally real to my vision – people in the community pulling together, combining skills to make it all work."*

This was Gwen's dream. What's yours?

TINYTOTS VISION CENTRE, SALFORD:

gwen.rolfe@greatplaces.org.uk

DREAM YOUR DREAM ...

> "The interesting and challenging thing about *Sing London!* is that it's never been done before. So it's a matter of holding on to your dream and making it up as you go along. Talk to lots of people... and get their feedback. This will help make your good idea a better idea. Then put it down on paper, when it will start to become real."
>
> **COLETTE HILLER**

Colette Hiller is an unstoppable American living in London. Her big idea was to get the whole of London singing during ten days in June 2007. She had been a stage- and film-actress – her high point being the role of Corporal Ferro in the cult movie *Aliens*. After moving to London, she produced radio programmes for the BBC, wrote and performed children's songs and actively campaigned against tower blocks in her neighbourhood.

Colette's idea came to her when organizing a sing-along at an older people's home. After singing for ten minutes, most of the audience had fallen asleep. Undiscouraged, she tried more familiar songs: "Pack up your Troubles"; "A Bicycle made for Two"; "We'll Meet Again". The audience woke up and joined in. As they sang, their spirits lifted and for a little while at least, they forgot their dreary surroundings.

For Colette, this was an epiphany – she realized that shared song had the power to reach across ages and cultures, and to make people feel happy. She decided that she wanted to bring one city together in song.

Her dream was to:

Reach all kinds of people ... *young people, old people and the "I can't sing" people ... the serious, the curious and anyone who sings in the bath ...*

With all kinds of music ... *from gospel to musicals, R & B to folk ...*

In all kinds of places ... *from theatres to department stores, in swimming baths and on the buses ... all ending with a Giant Finale in a prominent public place.*

...AND THEN MAKE IT HAPPEN

That was Colette's dream. She called her event *Sing London!* Nothing quite like it had been done before, at least not on this scale. To turn it into reality, all she needed to do was to get everybody to join in, create some unusual events such as *Singing Flashmobs* and *Complaints Choirs* (which would attract lots of publicity), and find enough money for the organizing costs.

Colette's simple idea together with an infectious enthusiasm captured people's imagination. People saw that it was do-able. They saw that all sorts of groups might be persuaded to participate . . . schools, church choirs, music societies, concert halls, opera houses, TV, celebrities, homeless groups, prisons . . . And when they were asked, they wanted to be part of it.

Like many good ideas, *Sing London!* has legs. Get it started, and it'll run. Why not *Sing Liverpool!* or *Sing Olympics!* or *Sing the World!*

Colette has already been approached by the City of Liverpool. She is in touch with the culture supremo for the London 2012 Olympics, who is strongly interested. And as for the whole world, that is sure to happen sometime!

Today, get yourself off to a good start. Sing a song in the bath, hum a tune on the bus on the way to work. If you're feeling blue, cheer yourself up – listen to the Coke commercial: **www.geocities.com/matty007ca/coke.html**

FIND OUT ABOUT *SING LONDON!*:

www.singlondon.org

PROBLEMS, PROBLEMS ...

If you are still stuck for ideas for what to do, check out this list. Think about whether there is a problem that particularly interests you. If there is, this may provide you with your starting point:

Children's rights

- Street children and runaways
- AIDS orphans
- Child prostitutes and child soldiers
- Child physical and sexual abuse
- Child slavery

Community

- Your dull and dreary neighbourhood needs cheering up
- Few opportunities for engaging in artistic and cultural activity
- Graffiti and vandalism
- Street homelessness
- Gang culture and antisocial behaviour
- The ageing population and all their problems

- Housing issues
- Threatened buildings and inappropriate redevelopment
- Streets no longer fit for people
- Infrequent, unreliable, dirty and expensive public transport.
- A complete lack of local distinctiveness

Conservation

- The destruction of the rainforest
- Endangered species
- Polluted rivers, oceans and beaches
- Big dams
- Disappearing languages

Democracy

- Low voter turnout
- Corrupt, lazy and uncaring politicians
- Public apathy on key issues

Discrimination

- The rights of people with disabilities
- Racism and sexism wherever it exists in society
- Gender violence and unequal opportunities for women
- Unequal rights for gay and transsexual men and women
- Islamophobia and religious intolerance
- Refugees and asylum seekers
- Animal rights and animal cruelty

Education and young people

- The right to an education
- School improvement
- Illiteracy and lack of books
- Bullying in schools
- No constructive activities for engaging young people
- Sex education and teen pregnancy
- Drugs awareness

Enterprise and cooperation

- Cooperatives and social enterprises
- Unemployment and lack of opportunity
- Skills and loans for people's livelihoods
- Ownership of intellectual property
- The power of multinational companies
- Corporate social responsibility
- The principles of CopyLeft and Open Source
- Internet access and a wired world

Environment

- Sustainable one-planet living
- The three Rs: Reduce, Reuse, Recycle
- Green electricity and solar energy
- Water consumption and drought
- Plastic bags and over-packaging
- Global warming and carbon emissions
- Pollution
- Pesticides and toxic waste
- Traffic and travel

Ethical consumption

- Consumerism and shopping
- Ethical banking and shopping
- Fairtrade and sweatshops
- Fast food and slow cities
- Grow your own

Health around the world

- Maternal and child mortality
- AIDS, malaria and other global diseases
- Medical research to solve today's and tomorrow's health problems
- Health and hospitals in the developing world
- Blindness and deafness
- Diabetes, cancer and heart disease
- Drug abuse
- Blood and organ donation
- Tobacco and smoking

Healthy living

- Veganism and vegetarianism
- Food miles and the food chain
- Genetic modification
- Mental illness and personal wellbeing
- Unhealthy lifestyles and obesity

Human rights

- Freedom of information
- Freedom of expression, freedom of the press
- Human wrongs around the world
- Torture
- The rights of prisoners and the victims of crime
- The death penalty
- Prisoners of conscience
- Refugees, asylum seeking and people trafficking

International development

- The Millennium Development Goals
- Third World trade, aid and debt
- Population
- Tools and equipment for the poor world
- Appropriate technology
- Hunger and food security
- Water and sanitation

Peace

- Conflict around the world
- Genocide and ethnic cleansing
- The arms trade
- Landmines

... SO WHAT'S YOUR PROBLEM?

1. Decide the problem you are going to tackle.

Think about all the issues that really concern you, which you think are important enough for you to do something about. Then write down the one issue that's most important to you. This is what you are going to work on.

2. Find out as much as you can about the problem.

Get hold of facts and figures. See what others are doing. Visit projects. Talk to people.

3. Decide what might be the best way of dealing with the problem.

You might, for example:

- **Do something in your own life, which will make a difference.**
- **Get publicity about the issue and start to raise public awareness that something needs doing.**
- **Force whoever is responsible to do something that will make things better.**
- **Campaign to get the law or the rules changed.**
- **Raise money, which you can then give to an organization or an individual who is prepared to do something.**
- **Enable those directly affected by the problem to do something. Work with them to help them see what they can do.**
- **Create your own solution. Come up with your own idea for a project. And then start to make it happen.**

NOW YOU ARE READY TO GET STARTED ON WORKING OUT WHAT EXACTLY YOU ARE GOING TO DO.

Chapter 4

Come up with a solution

If there's a problem, there must also be a solution. Think creatively and come up with your very own world-beating idea for dealing with the problem. If you have a great idea, then making things happen becomes a whole lot easier.

HOW ARE YOU GOING TO TACKLE THE PROBLEM?

You've decided what the problem is; now you need to decide what to do about it.

Try to come up with an imaginative solution. Something that is not only effective in addressing the problem, but which is both reasonably simple and cost-effective, which will create a sense of excitement, and where you can make use of your skills and talents.

If you're short on ideas, here are some exercises you can do to get your creative juices flowing:

1. Please yourself

What gives you a lot of pleasure? How you can use what pleases you to change the world?

1.Write down your ten main pleasures in life.

2.Write down one way of using each of these pleasures to address the problem.

3.Then select one thing to do. Do it. Enjoy yourself!

If you care about the environment, join a Green Drinks group, and enjoy a drink in a pub whilst discussing ideas for a better world. **www.greendrinks.org**

Sign up with Act for Love. This is a dating site for activists with the slogan "Take action, get action!". Change the world *and* meet your match. Sadly, it's for Americans only! **www.actforlove.org**

2. Do what you are good at

Identify your skills. Then think about how you can apply them to changing the world. You can achieve much more by using your brain than by simply emptying your wallet.

1. Write down six skills that you have.

2. Write down one way of doing something about the problem which uses each of these six skills.

3. Select one thing to do. Do it well.

3. Brainstorm a solution

Brainstorming is where a group meets to think up some good ideas; the more ideas, the better. Every idea is logged. Each should be stated in a few simple words. It should not be explained or criticized at this stage. One idea can lead to another.

The ideas that are generated can then be grouped together and discussed. Your aim is to identify a few ideas that appear to have real merit, which can either be explored further or put into action.

Brainstorming works well if there is an enthusiastic facilitator to encourage the flow of ideas. Do not worry overmuch if there is an occasional silence. People might be thinking. If the tempo is flagging, then the facilitator can throw in some wild ideas or select some of the seemingly better ideas so that these can be brainstormed further.

4. Go from problems to solutions to results

Explore the problem using a process called POSNAR

(after the initial letters of the six stages):

1 **Problem:**
State the problem. Explore all its different aspects. Think carefully about what causes the problem . . . and the cause of that.

2 **Objectives:**
Discuss some ambitious but realistic goals for doing something. What is your wildest dream for how things might be?

3 **Solutions:**
Think of the possible ways of achieving your objectives. What could you do if you had unlimited resources? Select an idea for a solution that's imaginative but feasible.

4 **Needs:**
If you are to be effective, set out your needs: good information, time to sort things out, people to help you, specific skills, materials, equipment, money.

5 **Action:**
What are the first steps you will take? Who will do what and when? How will the project evolve? What obstacles might you encounter? How will you overcome them?

6 **Results:**
How will you tell if you are doing OK? How will you know if you have succeeded? Or when you have failed?

5. Have a soak in a hot tub

The bath is a great place to relax. Mull over your problems as you soak in the hot water. As you begin to relax, ask yourself a sensible question . . . and see if you can come up with an imaginative answer.

Many of the techniques described here were developed by Nicholas Albery, social inventor, for his *Problem Solving Pocket Book*.

IF YOU'RE STILL STUCK . . .

If you're still stuck for ideas for how to get started, why not use chance to decide what to do?

Random information:

Access a piece of random information on the Internet:

• Read a random Wikipedia encyclopedia entry:
http://en.wikipedia.org/wiki/Special:Random

• Get some random information from the BBC's Guide to Life, the Universe and Everything:
www.bbc.co.uk/dna/h2g2/RandomEditedEntry

Does this information spark off any ideas?

Random numbers:

Generate a random number between 1 and 366 on the Internet at:

www.random.org/nform.html

Then get a copy of *365 Ways to Change the World* and go to the page with the same number; do the action for that day.

Roll the dice twice.

First, to choose from a list of six themes. And then, to choose from a list of six types of action. Make up your own lists, or use these:

Themes:

1. Conserving the environment

2. Fighting for human rights

3. Alleviating global poverty

4. Addressing global warming

5. Brightening up your community

6. Promoting peace

Actions:

1. Spend £10 of your own money

2. Volunteer two hours of your time

3. Write a letter to a newspaper

4. Think up a brilliant idea

5. Persuade five people to give you £5 each

6. Lobby your elected representative*

*IN THE UK USE THE WEBSITE:

www.writetothem.com

CREATING A HOLOCAUST MEMORIAL

If you can come up with a great idea, then this could provide you with the momentum you need . . .

The Paper Clips Project started with a really simple idea: 6 million Jews were killed in the Holocaust. In 1998, eighth-grade schoolchildren in Whitwell, Tennessee, wanted to get some idea of the size of what "6 million" looked like, and at the same time address issues of hate and intolerance. They had learned that Norwegians had worn paper clips on their lapels during the Second World War as a protest against the Nazi occupation.

So the children decided that they would collect 6 million paper clips – one for each Jew who was killed in the Holocaust – and then use these paper clips to create a monument to the Holocaust.

All the students started bringing paper clips. More were collected through an appeal on the school's website, from a letter-writing campaign and through the publicity that the project generated.

A steady stream of paper clips soon became a deluge. The final number of paper clips collected was approximately 30 million!

Two well-wishers, Peter Schroeder and Dagmar Schroeder Hildebrand, found and purchased a cattle wagon which had actually been used to transport Holocaust victims to the death camps. The story of how this was brought from Europe to Whitwell is told on the website. The students lined the wagon with Plexiglas and placed eleven million of the paper clips inside to honour the lives of all the people who had been murdered by the Nazis – gypsies, homosexuals, communists, Russians and others.

Eleven million more paper clips were used to create a monument to honour the children of Terezin (Theresienstadt); 144,000 Jews were sent there – including many scholars, professionals, artists and musicians. Inmates were allowed to lead creative lives. Concerts were held. The camp was landscaped with parks, flowerbeds and statues. But 33,000 died, mostly from hunger and disease, and 88,000 were deported to extermination camps.

The Children's Holocaust Memorial was opened in 2001. It includes more than 30,000 letters, documents and artefacts which were sent in by the public and catalogued by the students.

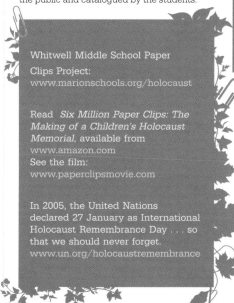

Whitwell Middle School Paper Clips Project:
www.marionschools.org/holocaust

Read *Six Million Paper Clips: The Making of a Children's Holocaust Memorial*, available from
www.amazon.com
See the film:
www.paperclipsmovie.com

In 2005, the United Nations declared 27 January as International Holocaust Remembrance Day . . . so that we should never forget.
www.un.org/holocaustremembrance

73

BECOME THE EXPERT

Once you have decided the issue you want to tackle, why not become an expert on the subject. This is actually quite easy. You just need to know just that little bit more than anyone else!

1. Choose a subject that you feel passionate about, preferably one where little adequate information is readily available. Stephen Millman, for example, wanted to know whether chocolate manufacturers used cocoa beans grown using slave labour.

2. Find out as much as you can about your chosen subject. Stephen wrote to all the confectionery manufacturers he could find to ask for information. Some replied willingly (these included manufacturers who were proud of their ethical record); some sent a rather bland meaningless statement; many did not bother to reply.

3. Publish the information.
Put it on a website. Stephen's website is **www.radicalthought.org**

4. Contact journalists and get as much publicity as you can, and also think up other ways of spreading the message – such as providing information for other people's websites. Your aim is to get known as "The Expert" on your chosen subject, so that when people need information or a comment, they turn to you.

5. Write an entry for the Wikipedia.
http://en.wikipedia.org

Even if plenty of information is already available on the subject, you just need to make sure that your information is better and more up-to-date.

The Cost of War project

In 2003, Niko Matsakis of Boston and Elias Vlanton of Maryland created **costofwar. com** which they ran for a year before handing it over to the National Priorities Project, which now hosts it.

You can find out the cost of the Iraq war to date for the USA and its citizens, both as a total cost and per person. You can compare the cost with the benefits that the money could have provided had it been spent instead on health, education, pre-school or housing.

The figures are based on Congressional appropriations. They include military and non-military spending on such things as reconstruction. Only incremental costs are included – the additional funds spent as a direct result of the war. For example, soldiers' regular pay is not included, but combat pay is included. Potential future costs, such as future medical care for soldiers and veterans wounded in the war, are not included. Nor is any deficit which will need to be funded from future appropriations.

http://costofwar.com/index.html

Iraq Body Count

The full extent of civilian deaths in Iraq goes largely unnoticed. Reports of incidents are scattered in different news sources and spread over time: one or two people killed here, a few dozen there. Only major incidents get headline coverage. But the numbers quickly add up.

General Tommy Franks, of US Central Command, was reported as saying *"We don't do body counts."* But the Iraq Body Count project does, and has achieved wide recognition as *the* authoritative source of information on civilian deaths in Iraq which have occurred as a result of the US-led invasion and subsequent occupation.

The Iraq Body Count was set up by Hamit Dardagan, a freelance researcher, and John Sloboda, executive director of the Oxford Research Group, which promotes non-military approaches to conflict resolution. The project is staffed entirely by volunteers and funded by public donations. They simply log news reports, but only where the information has appeared in at least two news services.

If you want to keep up to date on the latest figures, you can download the Iraq Body Count web counter on to your PC.

www.iraqbodycount.org

Sexism in the City

Scandals in the financial district often generate a huge amount of publicity, partly due to the high income levels of the people involved. Roy Davies, a librarian at the University of Exeter, and sister Linda Davies, a former merchant banker, have been documenting sexual harassment and sexism in London and New York, simply by providing references and weblinks to newspaper articles that have appeared on the subject.

www.exeter.ac.uk/~RDavies/arian/ scandals/behaviour.html

75

FROM PROBLEMS TO SOLUTIONS

Over the next few pages you will meet a number of people who are creating their own very individual solutions. They are doing it "their way".

Become a Secret Santa

In 1970, Larry Stewart was cold, hungry, jobless and homeless. It was a week before Christmas, and he had just been fired from his job. He walked into the Dixie Diner in Houston, Mississippi, without a dime in his pocket, and ordered a meal. When it was time to pay, he started looking for his wallet, pretending he had lost it. The owner of the diner, Ted Horn, realizing what was happening, took a $20 bill, came over to where Larry was seated, got down on the floor and peered under Larry's chair, and pointing to the $20 bill, said to Larry, *"This is what you were looking for – you must have dropped it."*

This act of kindness from a stranger changed Larry's life. He vowed that when he was in a position to help others, he would do it in a way that would also allow them to keep their dignity, as Ted had done to him.

Larry Stewart became a successful Kansas businessman, making millions from cable TV and telecoms. He made his first gift in 1979, at a drive-in restaurant. The attendant wasn't warmly dressed. "I think *I* got it bad. She's out there in this cold making nickels and dimes." He gave her $20 and told her to keep the change. "Suddenly I saw her lips begin to tremble and tears begin to flow down her cheeks. She said, 'Sir, you have no idea what this means to me.'" Larry went to the bank, took out $200, and drove around looking for people who could do with a lift. That was "my Christmas present to myself".

Every year since then in the weeks before Christmas, Larry has played "Secret Santa" and given away over $1.3 million. He started with $5 and $10 gifts, but now he hands out $100 bills, sometimes several at a time, to people in thrift stores, diners and parking lots. He kept his identity secret. But in 2006, after a course of chemotherapy, he decided to reveal himself and encourage others to become Secret Santas and shower the world with acts of kindness.

To become a Secret Santa, you just say, "I want to be a member of the Society of Secret Santas." There are no dues.

http://secretsantausa.com

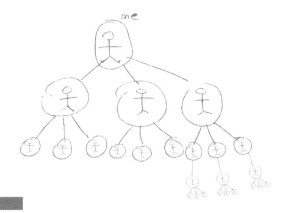

GIVE-IT-FORWARD-TODAY

In 2000 Catherine Ryan Hyde published a novel called *Pay It Forward* which became a Warner Brothers movie. In her novel, an extraordinary young man sets about changing the world through acts of kindness.

Alex Southmayd, an eighth-grade student from Boston, Massachusetts, was inspired by this, and set up the Give-It-Forward-Today (GIFT) foundation. This is what he says:

"Hi, I am Alex. My hobbies are sports, studying classical piano and trumpet, drama and singing. My favorite subjects in school are Latin, Physics, Math and English. Well, that's enough about me. I was inspired to begin this project after I read the novel and saw the movie, *Pay It Forward*.

"I thought it was great that one kid could really make a big difference in people's lives. One of the many things I have done to make a difference is to play the piano for the retired Sisters of Charity at a retirement home. I talk

with them after playing my music. Some of them feel forgotten by the world. I make sure to remind them of the wave of human kindness that they have created during their lives.

"When I was younger, my dad and I would play a game. We would try to do one good deed a day for someone. It was fun! *Pay It Forward* got me thinking how I could make this game bigger. I brainstormed ideas with my family, and the idea of GIFT was born.

"My dad once taught me that if you took a penny at the beginning of a month and doubled it every day, at the end of the month you would have over $5,000,000! What would happen if you did an act of kindness for only two people and you inspired those two people to make a promise and do an act of kindness for two other people? You would set in motion a wave of human kindness. This is the mission of GIFT."

GIVE-IT-FORWARD-TODAY:
www.giveitforwardtoday.org

BRINGING PEACE TO THE WORLD

Most of us are not going to bring together the Israeli and Palestinian leaders to agree to new Oslo accords. Nor are we going to be able to do much to influence the Sudan government about Darfur. And few of us are prepared to act as human shields when the next Iraq happens.

But there are lots of things that we can do to promote peace in the world. Here are two people doing unusual things for peace.

Peace Oil

Hilary Blume [left] came up with the idea for an olive oil that was produced by Jews, Arabs, Druze and Bedouin in Israel working together, and sold to generate profits for peace initiatives in the region. The oil is grown in the foothills of the Carmel Mountains. The olives are pressed within hours of picking. The prize-winning extra virgin olive oil is sold in bottles designed by Pearce Marchbank, one of the UK's leading designers. Peace Oil was launched in 2006 and was an immediate hit with consumers. It could be the first of a range of "peace products" produced in war zones or by communities in conflict.

www.peaceoil.org

A love-in for peace

"I'm just a normal person who lies in bed and protests against war. I'm not a hippy; I'm not a member of CND; I'm not a member of anything. But the issue is very serious, and you've got to take a stand sometime.

"It all happened on the eve of the Iraq war on St Valentine's Day 2003. In our tiny bedroom, we staged a John & Yoko-style love-in. We thought that we would send a photo of the two of us making the peace sign to our local newspaper.

"But a friend tipped off the BBC *Look North* programme, and we were asked to do a live interview from our bed. We asked other couples to join our protest, and help us make St Valentine's Day a day of love and peace. Several couples said they would join us. Someone even called us asking us to do a blue movie!

"After the interview, another friend took a picture of us in bed, which we e-mailed with a short press release to the local and regional press. This created a media frenzy.

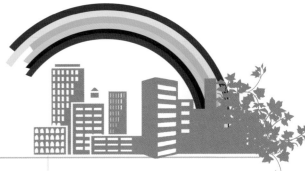

"We then received a strange phone call from someone called Murray Chalmers who told us he was from EMI. I got confused and thought he was from MFI (the flatpack furniture warehouse), and said that we didn't need any new furniture! But he insisted that he was from the record company and that he was Yoko Ono's publicist. I thought this was a practical joke, so took little notice of what he was saying. But it eventually dawned on me that he was Yoko's publicist."

"Yoko sent us a huge bunch of white lilies. Four camera crews turned up to film us in our bedroom, which is so small that they had to queue in the hallway to interview us. Photos appeared in the local and regional press. Our local newspaper described us as 'Nude Bed Protesters'. Our biggest worry was what our mothers would say! But they were more than supportive.

"We received several cards with poems and messages of support. A neighbour criticised us for wasting our time. From then on we knew we were doing something right, since no one kicks a dead dog!

"In March 2003, we did another love-in so that Yoko could telephone us – I didn't get a word in because Christine seemed to develop a natural rapport with Yoko. The BBC filmed this, but because of the war it wasn't fully screened. But it appeared on our local ITV programme. We were also interviewed by the late John Peel for the popular BBC Radio 4 programme *Home Truths*.

"In October 2003, we were invited to London to meet Yoko and attend John Lennon's DVD launch. We have fond memories of Yoko embracing us, saying 'At last we meet.' We felt honoured. I was subsequently approached by a news group to work as a freelance journalist. We still have contact with Yoko and Murray Chalmers. I even wrote a radio play about the event."

(Contributed by the love-in couple, Andrew and Christine Gale.)

Watch Andrew and Christine's video diaries made for BBC *Video Nations*:
www.bbc.co.uk/videonation/person/ gale_andrew

Hear the *Home Truths* interview:
www.bbc.co.uk/radio4/hometruths/ 0309bed_in.shtml

Andrew's next project is a mobile peace monument, which will travel around the world, spending one year in every capital city. It will act like a Nobel Peace Prize but given to countries to celebrate their contribution to peace and civil rights. His inspiration came from the Statue of Liberty, which was given to the United States by the French.

DOING SOMETHING ABOUT WATER

Reed Paget was attending a conference organized by the UN's Global Compact, which was seeking to get NGOs and multinational businesses to work together. Bill Clinton had pointed out that a quarter of the world's population did not have access to clean water. "I began asking myself whether I could do more than sit on the sidelines and point my finger at big business. What if I set up my own company and ran it from an environmentally minded point of view? After considering various grocery products, the idea of launching a brand of bottled water that would fund clean water projects sprung to life. What really appealed to me about this was its potential to raise awareness about an incredibly important issue as well as doing something to address that issue."

With fellow-American Marilyn Smith, Reed launched the Belu bottled brand in the UK in 2004. They sourced the water from a Shropshire spring and commissioned an award-winning design for their glass bottles. Belu still and sparkling water is distributed through the Waitrose and Tesco supermarket chains, and it is also sold to restaurants, clubs and offices. It was sold at the Live 8 concerts. In 2005,

> "When I was a teenager I expressed my environmental views through graffiti, when I was a bit older it was film making [he made the award-winning documentary *Amerikan Passport*], and most recently this concern for the planet has manifested in my setting up a bottled water company working to fund clean water projects."
>
> **REED PAGET**

Belu expanded its range to include water in a compostable plastic bottle made from corn. In 2006, Belu became the first bottled water *not* to contribute to global warming.

One hundred per cent of Belu's profits go to fund water projects in the developing world. Every bottle of Belu bought will provide clean water for one person for one month.

"I had a media communications background. But I didn't know what a financial model was, or a profit and loss statement, or a balance sheet, or a cash flow statement. I'd never read a business plan. I didn't really know the difference between marketing and advertising. I didn't know anything about sales, price, margin, bottle cap closures or pallet configurations. The list of the thousands of things needed to actually make something happen is pretty daunting." But Reed has shown that if you want to do something you can.

www.belu.org

Making a splash

Enterprising pupils at a British school are making a splash with their bottled water business and using their newly acquired business skills to bring life-saving water to an African village.

Sixteen pupils aged fourteen and fifteen at Fyndoune Community College in County Durham set up a business selling bottled water in school. They organized everything from buying to marketing and sales, and decided to donate the profits to build a well in Ghana. Their target was £3,000, which they achieved. They also approached businesses in the North-East to get support for a visit to Ghana to see for themselves what their profits were used for. Members of the group are now mentoring younger pupils who will keep the enterprise going.

They next want to address the issue of how the empty plastic bottles are disposed of. Having done a bit of research, they are pressing the local council to establish a recycling scheme.

But here is an even better business idea for them. The students collect the empty bottles, wash them, refill them with tap water and sell them! The profit margins would be huge, raising much more money for Ghana. No lorries would be needed to transport the water from the source to the bottling plant, to the distribution centre and then to you. It would also save on plastic. Everyone wins.

"People in Ghana often have to walk five miles to collect just one bucket of dirty water and we take water so much for granted here. Once we had decided we wanted to build a well then the idea of basing our business project on water seemed a good one." – Charlotte Burn, fifteen years old.

Just say Neau!

Neau is a brand of bottled water containing *no* water! The 33cl plastic refillable bottles are sold for the price of regular bottled water, with profits going to Third World water projects.

The bottle contains only a message telling people about the evils of bottled water – it's less fresh than tap, it could get polluted in the bottling plant, and then there are all the problems of energy use, pollution and congestion to deliver it to you. The leaflet advises you to fill up your Neau bottle with tap water. The Neau brand is ethical and as French-sounding as Perrier or Evian.

Neau was created in the Netherlands by an advertising agency called Vandejong – initially as a joke. But it's been so successful that they are now thinking of licensing the brand in other countries and also going into the water cooler business.

81

ENCOURAGING ETHICAL DRESSING

Here are four very different projects that promote ethical fashion.

Each aims to provide a practical solution to the problems of environmental sustainability and the sweated labour system – which brings us cheap clothes but at the price of low wages and poor working conditions for sweatshop workers around the world.

Find out more about sweatshops from:

www.nosweat.org.uk

www.maquilasolidarity.org/nosweat/cities/index.htm

www.coopamerica.org/programs/sweatshops

Fair trade school uniforms

One World Uniforms was founded by Katherine White and Jonathan Perera to produce school uniforms for the UK market, made from ethically sourced materials and dyes, manufactured according to fair trade principles with workers paid a wage that reflects the true cost of their work, and produced at each stage using sustainable methods of farming, manufacture and delivery.

This is a great idea for two reasons: there is a guaranteed demand for school uniforms, and it promotes the issue of fair trade to young people in a very practical way.

www.oneworlduniforms.co.uk

Worn Again clothing

"One evening in 2004 in a crowded nightclub, Anti-Apathy and Terra Plana met, fell in love and decided to make shoes together. Shoes for people who want good-looking feet, without a guilty conscience."

Cyndi Rhoades, founder of Anti–Apathy (see page 24), started the Worn Again fashion label for a big event on ethical fashion. She wanted to create new products from recycled materials.

The first products were a range of surplus military jackets customized by a small design company in Brick Lane, east London. Once you get started, one thing can lead to another. Cyndi met Galahad Clark, Director of Terra Plana and seventh generation of the Clark's shoe family, and they decided to collaborate on designing and producing a line of trainers to be used to generate income for Anti-Apathy. Terra Plana in its own words "aims to be the most innovative and sustainable designer shoe brand in the world".

Cyndi said "Yes," so long as the shoes were made from recycled materials and addressed key ethical issues.

Worn Again trainers are made from used suits, prison blankets. The shoes help reduce the tonnes of disused materials that end up in landfills and will hopefully stimulate demand for other products made from recycled materials.

www.wornagain.co.uk

www.terraplana.com

KNICKERS WITH A TWIST

Sarah Lucy Smith and Rose Cleary-Southwood were twenty-three-year-old Londoners who had been friends for years. They had started a sexual health clinic for teenagers whilst still at school. Sarah graduated in eco-design and then worked for top designer Zandra Rhodes. Rose got a degree in fashion merchandising and then worked with leading fashion labels Ted Baker, Principles and Burberry.

Sarah had developed the Green Knickers concept for her degree show. It aroused a lot of interest, and she started getting enquiries. So in 2005, Sarah and Rose decided to develop a business which would also promote ethical and ecological issues.

Green Knickers underwear is manufactured to Fairtrade standards and printed with slogans and designs which have a twist. Most of the range is made from silk or organic cotton or a cotton-hemp mix.

Other products include hemp-cotton padded cycling knickers to encourage cycling, and men's boxers.

The idea is great. The product is great. Perhaps they will do for lingerie what Anita Roddick did for cosmetics.

"What we bring is our own brand of revolution, using fun, humour, colour and sexy design. We aim to enchant our customers not with gimmicks and passing fashions, but with the real value of thoughtfully designed ethical products."

GREEN KNICKERS

The Green Knickers range includes:

- *Sensual Nature* showing solidarity with the environment (60 per cent hemp, 40 per cent silk): the leaves change from spring (green) to autumn (brown) and gradually fade away as the knickers are washed.

- *On Heat*, promoting awareness of global warming (100 per cent organic cotton): thermo-reactive pigments cause the sea to rise up and cover the land as the pants are warmed by body heat.

- *Understatements*: snazzy knickers with an embroidered slogan on the crotch saying "Eat Organic".

BUY YOUR GREEN KNICKERS AT:
www.greenknickers.org

83

SHOES FOR A BETTER TOMORROW

Buy one pair . . . and give another pair free . . . for a child in need.

TOMS Shoes are made to a traditional Argentinian design by Blake Mycoskie in Venice, California (Los Angeles) "to make life more comfortable". TOMS accomplishes this through its very special shoe and by donating one pair to a child in need for every pair purchased. This is Blake's story:

"I went down to Argentina for three weeks to play polo and to relax. A lot of the farmers and polo players wore these shoes called an 'alpagata' which has a rope sole and cardboard on the interior. They are the most comfortable shoes I have ever worn. A lot of the children in Argentina don't have shoes . . . and when they don't have shoes, they get cuts, they get scrapes, they get infected and it turns into a bigger health issue.

"I turned to my friend and I said I'm going to start a shoe company, it's going to be called TOMS – 'Shoes for Tomorrow' – and every pair we sell, we're going to give a pair to a

child in South America. We use a flip-flop-type bottom so that it would be urban and more comfortable, and we decided to have a leather insole so that your foot would stay dry if you wore them all day long out in the hot sun. We designed about fifteen different styles.

"I came back to the US and started giving them away to my friends and different celebrities. That was three months ago, and since then we have sold 5,000 pairs, we've been in half a dozen publications and it's just really exploded. I think right now in this environment there's a real opportunity for entrepreneurs who have social or environmental causes behind what they are doing.

"It's really important to us that we distribute the shoes ourselves in the different villages. Many of the kids had never received a gift before. So giving them shoes shows that someone cares about them. I realised that day that not only was TOMS going to help hopefully millions of kids by providing them with shoes, but we're also giving them hope.

"Don't ever let anyone tell you you can't do something because you have no experience. That is completely untrue. I had never been in the fashion business until three weeks ago. Now I have one of the fastest growing shoe companies in the world!"

TOMS shoes cost $38 a pair. You buy one pair, and they give another free. Buy two or more pairs and they are shipped free worldwide.

www.tomsshoes.com

WHY AREN'T THERE ANY TREES?

Imagine this scene. The central gutter in your roof is leaking, and an architect friend has volunteered to help you mend it. You've been to the building supply yard and bought a 4ft x 8ft sheet of zinc which you need to repair the gutter. You are carrying it back to your house. You are at the back, your architect friend is at the front.

Both of you notice that the street you are walking along needs a bit of cheering up. So you start chatting about what might be done.

You say: "Perhaps we should leaflet the houses and call a meeting. Then we can form a committee. I'm sure that the local Council has a grants fund for community initiatives. We could submit an application and get the money to buy some trees and all the equipment we'll need."

He says: "Nuts to that! I'll just borrow a pickaxe

and we can lift some paving stones. But before we do that, we'll plant some seeds in ice-cream tubs, and shower them with nutrients, water and lots of love until they're ready for planting out."

Whatever the problem, there will always be different ways of doing something about it. You may need lots of money to do it. Or you might be able to do it almost for free. You may want to set up some sort of formal structure. Or you might just want to take direct action and echo the Nike slogan *"Just do it!"*

There is no single right way of doing anything. What's best is what will work for you. But remember, you don't always need a lot of money (or even any) to make a difference.

IF YOU ARE INTERESTED IN PLANTING TREES, TREES FOR CITIES WILL TELL YOU HOW:

www.treesforcities.org

BRIGHTEN UP YOUR COMMUNITY

Something really extraordinary happened at Cavendish Gardens – all because of Graham Tuckley and Bob Wynn. It all began in 1995 at a party on the Beechdale Estate in Walsall held to celebrate the fiftieth anniversary of the end of the Second World War. Beechdale was a dreary and run-down place to live. The estate had just been transferred from Council ownership to a tenant-owned housing association.

A conversation led to the idea that Graham and Bob would do something about the gardens. The housing association made three conditions:

(1) that they get the permission of everyone;

(2) that they adopt the space as their responsibility to look after; and

(3) that they apply formally.

All this was done. An acer tree was planted to mark the occasion. Since then the estate has been modernized (pitched roofs, new windows, etc.), and the Cavendish Gardens part of the estate with 106 properties in an angle between an old railway line and a road abutting the M6 has been turned into the "garden capital of the West Midlands".

Under Graham and Bob's leadership, about twenty residents volunteer their time taking responsibility for the spaces outside their own flats (the estate is a mixture of two- and three-storey blocks, with some recently built bungalow housing for elderly residents). Cavendish Gardens is now a riot of colour – flowerbeds in bloom throughout the summer, lots and lots of window boxes and hanging baskets overflowing with flowers. There are lawns without weeds, sitting out areas with wooden benches and trellised covering, and much more.

Almost every property now has a magnificent garden, and the result is a wonderful neighbourhood where people actually want to live. There is a kitchen garden where flowering plants are grown to plant out in the gardens, and which produces free fruit and vegetables for the residents – salads, cucumbers, tomatoes, potatoes, runner beans peas, shallots, onions, leeks as well as soft fruit including grapes, raspberries, blackberries, rhubarb, and strawberries . . .

Each summer there is a barbeque to show off the gardens, entertain the residents and raise money for charity. In 2006, they organized a raffle, tombola, guess the weight of the cake and find the key competitions, bric-a-brac and cake stalls, a manicurist, face painting, candyfloss, and a swimming pool with music provided by a fairground organ. This result raised £1,000 for West Midlands Air Ambulance.

Graham and Bob set up a cooperative as the vehicle for doing all this. But this does not have money or even a bank account. Everything is done by people's own efforts, generosity and a shared community spirit.

The work continues. They now plan to raise the money to build a large conservatory-type building for use by residents, which will also provide day-care facilities for the elderly and disabled.

If you're passing by – it is moments from the M6 – take a detour and pay a visit. Or get yourself invited to their annual summer barbecue. Or just enjoy Cavendish Gardens from the comfort of your own home by visiting: **www.cgc.vze.com**

Going wild with flowers

Grant Luscombe also wanted to do something to put colour back into the environment. His big idea was to help local people transform derelict land by doing some simple soil preparation work and then planting simple mixes of common wildflower seeds. These would bloom to create a mass of colour and turn eyesores into urban parks. Grant established Landlife in 1975; and in 1996, he went on to create the National Wildflower Centre on Merseyside as a demonstration site and visitor centre.

LANDLIFE, FOR INFORMATION ON WILDFLOWERS:
www.landlife.org.uk and
www.wildflower.org.uk

NATIONAL WILDFLOWER CENTRE:
www.nwc.org.uk

87

TURNING IDEAS INTO ACTION

Here are some ideas which people are turning into action. They are all using their imagination and creativity to create solutions to problems in their communities and in the wider world.

Cycle Recycling:

Dave takes unclaimed stolen bikes and bike donations from the public and companies, then **repairs** and **recycles** them for use in low- income communities . . .

. . . which could be linked to **Cycling for Refugees**, where Jean Claude organizes an exercise programme involving cycling in parks which aims to counter obesity caused in part by stress and poor diet.

The Haven:

Terry is converting a house she inherited to provide flats for three women and their children plus community space for such things as baby massage, craft projects and IT training.

In the Can:

Deirdre organizes evening classes in film-making for inmates and staff at Wandsworth prison in London.

Used Car Apprentices:

Ali takes two groups of unemployed youths, one buys used cars, the other does minor repairs and sells them. The groups then exchange roles.

Weir Power:

Helen and Stephen are installing water turbines at weirs on rivers to generate electricity and provide a focal point for environmental education.

What's on in West Yorkshire:

Jean produces a monthly guide which provides information about what's on and encourages locally organized events.

The Story of Cradley Heath:

Harold is producing a short film about the history and people of a small village in the West Midlands as a means of strengthening community awareness and participation.

Off the Wall

Bijal provides graffiti art training for young people to channel their creative energies into something less anti-social than spraying walls.

Boxing and Brains:

Based on the idea that fighting is done in the ring and wars are waged in the boardroom, Eliezer provides training in boxing, entrepreneurship and IT skills.

Look and Listen:

Nick is developing a toolkit for people living in small towns and villages to produce a downloadable audio-visual tour of their community for visitors, which could be used to promote the town and encourage local tourism.

Eco-Rentals

Rabab is converting property for low-impact living to include features such as solar energy, wind power, water harvesting and insulation, which will be rented out.

Glass Creations:

Hywel uses recycled glass to make and sell a range of products, including coasters, lamps and clocks.

Basic Bricklaying for Beginners:

Antony and David run a short course providing bricklaying skills for some do-it-yourselfers and a new career for others.

LIGHTING UP THE WORLD

More than a third of the world's people live without access to electricity.

The arrival of dusk brings darkness into many people's lives – no chance for children to do homework or for adults to engage in some activity which will generate additional income. Education and livelihoods suffer.

Can renewable energy light a path to a new dawn? Two MBA students, Amit Chugh and Matt Scott [shown above], thought so. Inspired by the Light Up the World Foundation, they decided to give it a go. They set up Cosmos Ignite Innovations with the vision of "empowering lives through innovative products".

Their first goal was to remove darkness from homes without light and provide a safer, cheaper alternative to the widely used kerosene oil lamps. Using existing technologies, they designed the Mighty Light, a solar-powered low-maintenance lantern that uses a LED bulb, which delivers four times more light output than other bulbs. It can hang from the ceiling or be used as a torch. It has a narrow-focused beam, or can be adjusted to emit diffuse light. "It is our first step . . .".

www.cosmosignite.com
www.lutw.org

WHAT'S YOUR BIG IDEA?

Margaret Thatcher, British Prime Minister for much of the 1980s, once said of one of her cabinet ministers, "I like him because he brings me solutions." We may all be aware of the problems. But if you can come up with a creative solution, this can be a great starting point for your efforts to change the world.

The case of the used batteries

Batteries contain lots of toxic chemicals and should not be thrown out with the rubbish – they will end up in a landfill, and all the dangerous chemicals will leach out into the soil and into the water table.

The batteries in your torch have just run out, and you can't find anywhere local where you can leave your batteries for recycling. Do you:

1. Throw your batteries in the rubbish, because you can think of nothing better to do?

2. Put your battery to one side hoping an opportunity turns up? But after a few weeks, nothing has happened. So you absent-mindedly or deliberately toss the batteries into the rubbish bin.

3. Tell everyone you meet how difficult it is to recycle batteries, hoping that someone will come up with a suggestion?

4. Write a letter to your local newspaper, in the hope that you will find other people who have the same problem? Together you can form a group to press for something to be done.

5. Do something to solve the problem. You might try to persuade the manager of your local supermarket to place a battery recycling point between the checkout and the car park, and promise to arrange to take away the batteries on a regular basis. You point out that this could get the supermarket a lot of good publicity as well as encourage people to shop there.

6. Aim much higher and try to change the world. You have a vision of battery recycling points all over the country. Your first recycling point in your local supermarket is your first step towards achieving this.

In the UK, about 22,000 tonnes of batteries are thrown away each year. That's a heck of a lot.

...AND WHAT ARE YOU GOING TO DO ABOUT IT?

Now it's crunch time. It's no good just having a good idea. You have to put your time and energy into making your idea work. You have to go out and do something. The next chapter will show you how to get organized, how to communicate your ideas effectively, and how to get the resources you will need to change the world.

TO FIND OUT ABOUT BATTERIES, VISIT THE BATTERY UNIVERSITY AT

www.batteryuniversity.com

Chapter 5

Go out and do something

Start your own project. Find others who will work with you to make something happen. It can be a lot of fun. You will make a difference, and you will make new friends. It could even change your life.

GET ORGANIZED

You've come up with a great idea for changing the world. Now you need to do something about it. What you do next is crucial. Take the first step, and you're on your way. Fail to take it, and your great idea will remain just that – a great idea, nothing more.

But it's not always easy to take that first step. All sorts of things might be holding you back:

- **Self-doubt:**
  "It seemed like a good idea at the time. But I've thought a bit more about it, and I'm not so sure."

- **Fear of failure:**
  "It sounds great, but I really don't think it will work."

- **Fear of being laughed at:**
  "How can my idea be important? I'm just little me. All those experts and big organizations out there know much more about it than I do."

- **Lack of resources:**
  "It needs lots of money to do it. And I haven't a bean."

Don't worry about any of this. When you thought up the idea, your instincts told you that it was a great idea. Now give it a try. With energy and commitment, do your best to make it work. If it does, that's great! If not, you will have learnt a lot from the experience . . . and you'll do better next time.

Here are three things to help you move your idea forward:

1. Talk to plenty of people about your plans. Talk to experts. Talk to people who have done something similar. Talk to your friends. Go up and talk to someone in a bookshop or the person sitting next to you on the bus. Their ideas and feedback will be useful to you. You will also be making a statement to yourself and publicly that you are determined to go ahead.

2. Find one or two people who are prepared to help you. You will no longer be doing it on your own. You will have people to discuss your hopes and your fears, people who will encourage you and who will help you through what could be difficult times.

3. Draw up an action plan. Make a list of the first five things you must do to get started. Then do all five.

Once you've got started, it will all become much easier. You are on your way. One thing will lead on to another. And a momentum will build up.

Taking the first steps

Think about what you need to do to turn your idea into action. More research, developing useful contacts, getting some publicity for the idea, exploring the possibilities for getting funds, producing some explanatory literature, designing a pilot project, finding people to help you, forming some sort of committee . . .

Write down the first five things that you will do once you have decided to go ahead.

CREATING THE MUSLIM YOUTH HELPLINE

After completing a course in counselling and youth work, seventeen-year-old Mohammed Mamdani established the Muslim Youth Helpline with a group of friends to provide advice to teenage young Muslims growing up in a world of confused values.

In September 2001, Mohammed installed a telephone line in his bedroom, obtained an email address, joined the Telephone Helplines Association to get information on relevant policy and legislation, got some publicity for the project, organized a rota for answering the phone calls, and sat back and waited for the calls to come through.

And come through they did. There were a lot of young people facing the usual problems that young people face as they grow up (relationships, bullying, stress and health, rows with parents, etc.), but also problems particular to them as young Muslims (Islamophobia,

fundamentalism, arranged marriages, the more conservative values of the older generation, etc.).

Money was a problem initially. Mohammed's father paid the telephone bill; family and friends dipped into their pockets. Having proved a huge need, Mohammed and his team went on to raise £16,000 towards an office, and then recruited and trained a team of young volunteers with first-hand experience of the issues and problems facing young Muslims in the UK today.

Advice is provided by telephone, email and via the website, and also through an online magazine called muslimyouth.net. At first, the scheme operated in Greater London. It has since gone nationwide.

www.myh.org.uk
www.muslimyouth.net

Here is how Michael Norton got started on two projects . . .

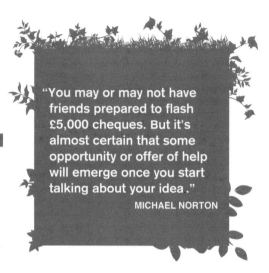

365 WAYS

"You may or may not have friends prepared to flash £5,000 cheques. But it's almost certain that some opportunity or offer of help will emerge once you start talking about your idea."

MICHAEL NORTON

In 2002, I set up an international summer school for young activists. The 250 or so young people from all over the world were bubbling with ideas for how to make the world a better place. Inspired by them and what they were doing, I thought that it would be a great idea to write a book suggesting small actions that people could take in their own lives and in their communities to make a difference. I had a vision for the book. It would be jam-packed with interesting information and inspiring case studies of people who had done something. It would present changing the world as a lot fun, and ideally spur people into wanting to make a difference . . .

That was in July 2003. I then began to have doubts. I had never written the sort of book that was sold in bookshops. Nobody would be interested in publishing it. It would be a huge amount of work, and I was just too busy. I kept thinking up reasons for not going ahead.

But I did talk to people about the idea. They all seemed to like it. In May 2004, two friends actually offered to do something to help me

take it forward. Stephen, a lawyer, offered me £5,000 from his small family trust to pay for a researcher. Vicki, a Canadian who was also involved in encouraging youth action, suggested we go into partnership: she would do the website if I did the writing and found a publisher. She would have a 50 per cent stake in the enterprise. On the basis that working with someone is easier than working alone, and that half of something is worth a whole lot more than all of nothing, I agreed.

I hired a young researcher for three months. We set up a network of volunteer contributors, ran ideas workshops and created the first hundred ways to change the world. After that I had to complete the project on my own. But I'd got started. That was the important thing.

365 Ways to Change the World was originally published in December 2005. Vicki withdrew from the project in March 2005 due to other commitments.

www.365act.com

YOUTHBANK

The idea for YouthBank came to me in November 1997 whilst walking on a beach in Devon. I was discussing how school students could get the funds they needed for the community projects they were organizing as part of their citizenship education programmes. Mostly they needed only quite small amounts. If they wrote to local grant-makers or companies, it often took too long to get a decision, by which time term might have ended or exams were looming. They needed money, and they needed it now!

So I thought about setting up a Challenge Fund, where young people could apply and get a quick decision. I then thought that such a fund *should be run by young people*. The young grant-makers would create the grants policy, make decisions on what to support, and be responsible for ensuring that the money under their control is used effectively.

Giving young people the responsibility for making real decisions with real money provides an amazing learning opportunity. And the chances are that they will make better decisions, as they knew more about the issues that concerned young people. It seemed a really good idea.

Nothing quite like this had been done before, although a bit of research showed that there were some philanthropy training programmes for young people in the USA (such as the Michigan Young Grant-makers).

What was my next step? I wrote a two-page concept paper, which I circulated to around fifty foundations, companies, leading youth organizations and a few people whose judgement I trusted. I invited them to attend a meeting in February 1998 to discuss the idea.

Thirty people turned up. Five volunteered to be part of a steering committee – they included representatives from a number of national youth agencies. I invited them to help me work out how to turn the idea into practice. And just as importantly, a foundation had faxed me two weeks earlier to say that they could not attend, but that they would like to offer a substantial sum for young grant-makers to distribute. We were now on our way.

Eight years later, there are around seventy YouthBanks across the UK, and the idea is spreading internationally.

Remember this. Foundations get far more applications than they can fund, but they are always on the look out for good ideas. Your idea might be just right for them!

www.youthbank.org.uk

97

ADVICE ON GETTING STARTED

Reed's advice
Reed Paget is the creator of Belu Water *(page 80)*.

Be creative: If you've got no cash and need to get something done, read a book, learn how to do it yourself, then do it yourself.

Be confident: With your good idea, nothing is impossible. You just have to believe in yourself.

Use free help: Help can come in all forms – for us it included financial advice, branding and packaging design and even free office space. Make a list of what you need.

Be prepared to make sacrifices: The impact of two or three years working seven-day weeks is a kind of glazed look permanently fixed on your face. If I had a normal job, I would have savings, take holidays, maybe own a house or a car. But I don't have any of these things. But I feel comparatively blessed.

Sarah's advice
Sarah created Green Knickers *(page 83)*

Be passionate:
If you are, the energy that you channel into your project can make you unbeatable. But the quality I value most is optimism. This optimism is present in my life, in my dreams, in my products. The reason I try is because I believe I will succeed.

Cyndi's advice
Cyndi is the founder of AntiApathy *(page 24)* and Worn Again trainers *(page 82)*

Be open to new ideas: Never get stuck in your beliefs. Have an open and evolving mind. The realities of the world are constantly shifting.

The qualities you need to change the world: passion, curiosity, open-mindedness, business sense, flexibility, drive, endurance, belief, trust, support, encouragement, enjoyment, persistence and fulfillment. I developed all of these as my project progressed.

Graham's advice

Graham is the moving spirit behind Cavendish Gardens *(page 86)*

Be unstoppable: Bureaucracy wants to nip projects in the bud even before they have got off the ground. They find it easy just to say "No" to everything. They can create unnecessary barriers. Believe strongly in what you are doing; don't get put off by the difficulties you encounter.

Make use of other people's skills: People like to be asked to help, especially if they have a skill you really need. Remember to thank them and to praise them for what they have helped you achieve.

Philippa's advice

Philippa Long set up TIE to provide communications expertise to NGOs in developing countries

Get other people on your side: If you're passionate about something and believe in it 100 per cent, people will listen to you, take you seriously and do everything they can to help make your dream a reality.

Things often tend to take a little longer to get sorted than you originally anticipate . . . so be easy on yourself if you miss your targets.

The qualities you need to change the world: Passion, enthusiasm, determination, courage in your convictions, gift of the gab, networking, emotional intelligence, leadership, empathy, understanding, listening and being flexible and open-minded.

Mark's advice

Mark set up the Wellbeing Project *(page 176)*

Think outside of the box: Challenge convention; don't just accept that things have to be done in a particular way, just because they've always been done that way.

Go out and make your own luck: Present your work at meetings, conferences, talk about your project anywhere and everywhere. Get people excited about what you want to achieve.

Jason's advice

Jason Loughlan is an eco-designer

I live by this quote:

"Anything you dream you can create."

ALBERT EINSTEIN

ACTION GUIDE: GETTING ORGANIZED

1.
WHAT DO YOU WANT TO DO?

You have your own reasons for wanting to do something, for wanting to set up a project (or even start a new organization). Before you get started, it is important to be very clear about what you are proposing to do. This will give you a sense of "Mission". It will make everything much easier.

Here are some of the things that you might want to think about. If you answer all these questions in plain English – avoid using jargon at all costs – then you will have got yourself a **Mission Statement** which explains why your project exists and what you hope to achieve.

Question 1: What's the problem that concerns you?

Describe the problem or the need or the issue *as you see it:*

_____

_____

_____

_____

_____

_____

_____

_____

Question 2: What's your dream for a better future?

Your "dream" is a great starting point. It will inspire you to action, guide you as you go along and help you through hard times. Write down your dream. Use it as a Vision Statement to inspire others to join with you:

_____

_____

_____

_____

_____

_____

_____

_____

_____

_____

_____

Question 3: What do you want to achieve?

Your prime reason for doing something is to make some sort of impact on the problem. Think about what you actually want to achieve through your efforts:

_____
_____
_____
_____
_____
_____
_____
_____
_____
_____
_____

And now set out some clear simple aims of your project:

_____
_____
_____
_____
_____
_____
_____
_____
_____
_____
_____
_____

Question 4: What are your values?

Are you committed to user involvement or equal opportunities and inclusiveness? Or to putting human rights or environmental sustainability at the heart of what you are doing? Are there any strong ethical values that underpin your work?

_____
_____
_____
_____
_____
_____
_____

If values are important to you, make sure that you are clear what these are and that they are shared amongst everybody who is helping you make the project a success.

A Mission Statement should:

1. Express a sense of purpose for what the group is doing.
2. Be clearly understood by everybody.
3. Be short and punchy, and jargon-free.
4. Inspire everyone who is involved in helping take things forward or in giving support.

2. FINDING OUT A BIT MORE

What is the problem?

You need to really understand the problem, if you are to do something effective about it. Here are two things you can do right at the beginning:

- Talk to people who are affected by the problem. This could be the people you want to help. Or it could be the local community.
- Do some basic research. This could mean digging up some facts and figures. Or you might do you own needs survey.

List some of the reasons why you believe that the problem is important:

_____

_____

_____

_____

_____

_____

_____

_____

Why are you different?

Who else is doing something about the problem? You may find that there are lots of other people who are as concerned about the problem as you are, and who are doing all sorts of things to address it. It is important that you know about what else is happening. You may be able to learn from other people's ideas and experience. And if what you are doing is different, you will be able to explain what the differences are and the advantages of your approach.

List some of the organizations that are doing something similar, and explain what makes your project different and special.

_____

_____

_____

_____

_____

_____

_____

_____

_____

_____

_____

_____

_____

_____

_____

_____

3.
WHAT ARE YOU GOING TO CALL YOUR PROJECT?

Names:

The name you give your group or project is important. It sets the tone for what you do. It can be a lot of fun thinking about what to call yourselves. Come up with something really nice.

Names can be:

• **Descriptive**, such as Green Knickers, which produces underwear from sustainable fabrics.

• **Zappy**, such as Express Yourself Mums, which promotes breast feeding, or Off the Wall, which provides graffiti art workshops for young people to focus their energies and creativity, or In the Can, which organizes film-making classes in prisons.

• A **slogan** of some sort, such as Make Poverty History.

• An **acronym**, such as PETA, which stands for People for the Ethical Treatment of Animals.

So what's the name of your group going to be? Decide now:

_____

_____

_____

_____

Straplines:

A strapline expands on your name with a few more words which outline what you are trying to do. Your strapline can be used alongside your name on letterheads, leaflets and posters. Here are some examples:

• UnLtd: **The Foundation for Social Entrepreneurs**.

• WWF: **for a living planet**.

• World Social Forum: **Another world is possible**.

Think up a strapline for your project:

_____

_____

_____

_____

_____

_____

_____

_____

Here is a simple way of getting a constitution for your group. Just fill in the chart and get all your founding members to sign it.

1. What is the name of your group?

insert the name you wish to call your group

2. What is the purpose of your group?

insert what you have come together to do

4.
DRAWING UP A CONSTITUTION

3. Where is the area of your work?

insert your neighbourhood or community, your town or city, nationally or internationally

If you are a group of people working together on a project, it is important that there are some rules for how your group will operate.

Your constitution is the document where these rules are set out. You will need to provide a copy of this document when opening a bank account.

4. Who are your members?

insert the names of the founding members of your group, and the procedure for enrolling new members

Most constitutions are written in complicated and hard-to-understand legal language. But it is possible to produce something much simpler that everybody can understand.

5. How will new members of the group be appointed?

we suggest: by majority decision of existing members

6. How can members of the group resign or be removed?

we suggest: by resigning in writing at any time, or to be removed by a three-quarters vote of the members present after the member to be removed has been given notice of the meeting and an opportunity to talk at it

7. How will meetings be held and run:

How frequently

we suggest: weekly, fortnightly or monthly

How much notice to be given

we suggest: details of meetings and agenda to be circulated at least three days beforehand

Quorum for meetings

we suggest: at least three people must be present before any decision can be made

How decisions are made

we suggest: by majority decision with the person chairing the meeting having a casting vote in the event of a tie

Minutes of meetings

we suggest: the Secretary to take the Minutes and perhaps to circulate them within one week

8. What are your powers

we suggest: the group can do anything that is legal which will help it achieve its aims

9. How will annual general meetings be held

we suggest: an AGM with all members of the group invited should be held within three months of the end of the year to receive the accounts for the previous year, to review progress and to appoint or re-appoint the Honorary Officers for the coming year.

10. How will honorary officers be appointed

we suggest: at the AGM, the members shall vote for one member of the group to act as Chairperson (to chair meetings and take a leadership role), another to act as Treasurer (to keep the accounts), and a third to act as Secretary (to organize meetings and minutes). Members are invited to put themselves forward for election to these roles

11. How will your bank account operate

we suggest: the group can open a bank account to deposit surplus funds. Cheques should require two signatures

12. How will accounts be kept

we suggest: each month the Treasurer will prepare a statement of all payments made and all income received for the year so far, and within two months from the end of each year the Treasurer will prepare annual accounts

13. How will any surplus funds be used

we suggest: if the group wishes to disband or when it has completed all its work, any surplus funds will be donated to another group with similar aims

14. Signed by the founding members

Signed by:

Date:

A word of caution from a lawyer.

Please note that your constitution does not confer any protection on the individual members of the group. So if you are undertaking a substantial project or handling large sums of money, this may create obligations on you and result in liabilities if you fail to do what you promise. You should try to make sure that any claims can only be made against the group and paid for from its assets, and that no claims whatsoever can be made against the members of the group when they have acted in good faith. One way of achieving this is to set yourself up as a company.

Ready-made constitutions.

You may be able to get hold of a model constitution from a national body promoting community organizations. This can be a good idea if you are creating a formal organization which will continue.

5.
THE SKILLS YOU WILL NEED

Your personal skills

To make your project a success, you will need to be:

An enthusiast: You will need to motivate people to get behind you in all sorts of ways. An infectious enthusiasm will help you do this.

A creative thinker: Your great idea will ensure that your project is a success. And you need to bring your creativity into all aspects of your project.

A good planner: You have to be able to turn your idea into action, and then to make it work. And you have limited time and resources, which you will need to make best use of. Strategic thinking and careful planning will help you achieve what you want.

A problem-solver: You will encounter all sort of problems along the way. You need to be able to deal with them quickly and effectively.

An effective communicator. You will need to persuade people about the importance of your idea and to get them to support you. Good public speaking skills will help you achieve this.

A persuader: There will be all sorts of things you will need to ask people to do for you. In particular, you will need to get support in kind – this includes services and facilities as well as things. And you may need to lobby politicians and others to get policy changed.

A good administrator: You need to be practical and well organized. You should try to do things when you say you will and keep good records.

Think about your strengths and weaknesses. If you have a weakness, you can:

• **Learn as you go along.** You won't do everything right first time, but you will improve with experience.

• **Go on a training course.** This will take time and money, but it can be a good investment.

• **Find someone else to do it for you.** For example, if you know somebody who is really great at asking, then get them to do this for you.

6.
FINDING PEOPLE TO HELP YOU

There will be a number of other skills you need, where it is probably best to find other people who have these, and then ask them to help you:

Writing skills: You will need to produce well-written reports and newsletters. Try to find someone who has good writing skills (perhaps a journalist), and delegate the task to them of producing a newsletter.

Design: You will need to produce lively leaflets and posters. How these are designed will influence the way people see you.

IT skills: You will almost certainly need a website to promote what you are doing, encourage feedback, sell things and for online giving.

Fundraising: You will have to ask for money. You need to know who to ask and how to ask. But there will also be a lot of work to do in writing applications. If you can find someone to help you with this, it will make your fundraising a lot easier.

Accountancy: You have to keep accounts and prepare regular financial information to see how things are going. You may want to find somebody to do the basic bookkeeping and prepare quarterly and annual accounts.

Legal: You will need legal skills to help you set up an organization and obtain charitable status. This can be expensive. You might try to persuade an experienced lawyer to help you for free.

Make a list of all the skills you will need. Get a group of people around you who have these skills, and who will take responsibility for these aspects of your project.

Using volunteers

You may also need willing volunteers to help out, for such things as:

- Manning the office or answering the telephone

- Distributing leaflets and newsletters

- Helping collect money or organize a fundraising event

- Doing research on the Internet or through a survey

- Helping deliver your service (what your project was set up to do)

- General dogsbody work

A lot of people out there are looking for something meaningful to do, and may be prepared to help you as a volunteer. Your job is to find them . . . and then to make sure you use them effectively.

You need to do the following to make the most of your volunteers:

- Ensure that they share your values. If they don't, they may misrepresent what your project is about or it may cause friction.

- Give them a clear description of what you want them to do and the time it will take. Ask them to make a commitment to do this.

- Give them an induction into the work that your project is doing.

- Pay their out-of-pocket expenses (if you can).

- Be there to support them if they encounter any difficulties.

- Thank them.

- Praise them for what they have been able to achieve.

Involving users

It's always a good idea to consult with your beneficiaries – those people who will be benefiting from what you are doing – and with your local community. They will be able to give you useful insights from their perspective, and their input will strengthen your project.

For example, if you are . . .

Improving your neighbourhood: consult with local residents.

Working with young people: ask the young people for their ideas.

Helping the homeless: discuss your plans with your local Big Issue seller and other homeless people.

Developing a project in a village in India: do a house-to-house survey and then organize a meeting with the local community

---

You can involve users and your local community in the following ways:

- **On your board:** You can appoint one or more users as committee members.

- **On an advisory group,** where they can advise you from a user's or community perspective.

- **As volunteers or paid staff** (part time or full time), to help you deliver the project.

7.
PLANNING WHAT TO DO

Now it's time to start thinking about what you are going to do. You need to remember that you just don't have the time or the resources to do everything all at once. Here are some things to bear in mind:

• **Be ambitious:** You should want to stretch yourself. But don't set yourself overly ambitious targets. You don't want to set yourself up to fail.

• **Try to focus your efforts** on what will achieve real results and create momentum. Some things will be hard to make work, some will require a lot of resources (time as well as money), and some will not have that much impact.

• **Decide what you need to turn your plans into action:** the **people** to act as helpers, volunteers; the **premises and facilities**, and whether these are available; **equipment**, and whether you can borrow it or get it donated; **money**, and what more you will need to raise; and any **promotion or publicity** which will help you achieve your aims.

• **You need to have some successes** from time to time in order to keep up your morale – however small these successes might be.

• **It often takes far longer to achieve what you want.** Be prepared for this.

• **It will help if you set yourself milestones** – things that you will achieve along the way towards achieving your eventual aims. This will help you chart your progress. Set out what you want to achieve in the short term (the next three months), the medium term (the next twelve months), and the longer term (the next three years).

• **Don't get diverted.** In your plan, you will have decided what's important. Concentrate on this.

• **Things change . . .** new opportunities may arise, you may learn from experience what you can and can't do. So revise your plan from time to time.

• **Make one person responsible for each thing you are planning.** Make that person accountable for ensuring its success.

Plan for establishing a young person's banking project

Elisabetta Lapenna is setting up banks in schools which will be run by the students, to promote financial literacy, to encourage saving and give young people a hands–on opportunity to run a successful enterprise.

This was her nine–month action plan:

- Establish an advisory group: July

- Take advice and finalize the name and brand: July–Aug

- Take advice on banking and credit union law: July–Aug

- Finalize the concept and produce a leaflet: July–Sept

- Consult with schools and young people: Aug–Nov

- Create a blueprint for the pilot programme: Aug–Nov

- Write and produce a user's manual: July–Sept

- Set up three pilot projects in schools: Oct–Feb

- Identify future stakeholders (find six organizations who are interested being involved in Phase 2): Oct–Feb

- Develop a business plan for Phase 2: Dec–Jan

- Apply for funding for the second stage: Nov–Feb

- Organize a consultative event bringing together all interested parties (100 people): Feb–March

8. MEASURING YOUR SUCCESS

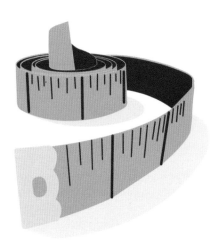

You should try to *monitor* **what is happening, by measuring the:**

- **Inputs:** These are the resources you put into the project to try to make something happen (the time, the money, the expertise and the equipment and facilities you need).

- **Outputs:** This is what you make happen. For example, 1,000 copies of a newsletter distributed, or thirty people attending a three-month training programme.

You should also try to *evaluate* **your effectiveness, by trying to measure the:**

- **Outcomes:** This is the effect on the beneficiaries. For a training programme, it could be an increase in skills and self-confidence. You should try to make sure you are measuring the right thing.

- **Impact:** This is the longer-term change that occurs as a result of what you have done. What will people do with their increased skills and self-confidence? It could be that they find full-time employment, and then go on to transform their lives.

You monitor and evaluate your project in order to:

- *Learn from what you have done*, so you do it even better next time.

- Show yourself and your funders that you are *using their money effectively.*

- Provide the evidence to *persuade more people to support you.*

Bear in mind the following:

- **Quality:** Some projects work with a lot of people; others work more intensively with fewer people. You should decide whether it is *quantity* of people or the impact on them that is your priority. But whatever you do, try to ensure that what you do is of high *quality.*

- **Cost-effectiveness:** Try to show that you are cost-effective – that you are using resources *efficiently* to create a lot of benefit.

Deciding what to measure

A Meals-on-Wheels service decided to evaluate their service. They knocked on doors and talked to some of the old people who were receiving meals. Everyone said how much they enjoyed the meals and how happy they were with the service.

But the evaluator also decided to look in the dustbins, where she often saw meals thrown away partly eaten or sometimes completely unopened. What the old people really liked was contact with the outside world and the chance of a chat, which seemed a lifeline for people who were largely housebound and often lonely.

You can learn a lot from evaluating what you are doing. With that knowledge you can go on to improve your project.

Who will do your evaluation?

• **You**, yourself: This will not be an independent evaluation. But it is often quite easy to collect the data yourself and try to assess your performance. You may want to take advice from someone more experienced on what to measure.

• **A professional evaluator:** You will probably need to pay someone to do this. For a large project or for something which you are planning to scale up, this may be the best option.

• **Your users or beneficiaries:** They can discuss what to measure and your ideas for undertaking the evaluation – after all it is their lives which are being changed.

What will you measure?

What you plan to achieve:

Outputs_____

_____

_____

Outcome_____

_____

_____

Impact_____

_____

_____

_____

9. HANDLING MONEY

Not all projects need money. But most do. You first have to raise the money you need. Once you have money, this will bring certain responsibilities:

1.You must ensure that the money is **kept safe.**

2. You should try to **earn as much interest as you can** on any unspent balances. This will increase the amount you have available to spend on your project.

3. You must ensure that the money is **spent only for the purposes for which it was given** to you. If it isn't, you will be "in breach of trust" – and this can destroy your reputation.

4. You should try to ensure that the money is used as **cost-effectively** as possible, so that you make as much of an impact as possible with the resources at your disposal.

How to keep your money safe

1. Don't keep too much cash lying around: It's best to put as much of your money as possible into a bank account, and then to pay your bills by cheque. Use petty cash only for very small transactions.

2. Make it a rule that any cheque requires two signatures, and that supporting documents are supplied when asking people to sign cheques. Under no circumstances should the second signatory sign a number of blank cheques in advance to make it easier to pay the bills.

3. Ensure that proper accounts are kept.

Opening a bank account

If your organization wants to open a bank account, it will require a formal committee resolution and you must supply a copy of your constitution along with the application form.

You can get application forms from your chosen bank. Check out the terms offered by different banks. Some will pay interest on any balances held, whilst enabling you to make withdrawals at any time. Some will pay no interest. Some will require you to give several months' notice if you want to make a withdrawal, or charge a penalty if you need to get hold of the money sooner. Some banks will charge you for each transaction; others may offer you "free banking".

If you have a large bank balance, you might wish to operate two accounts: an interest-bearing deposit account for long-term balances, and a current account for day-to-day transactions.

You might also want to use an "ethical bank" – one that is socially responsible in how it runs its business.

Take into account all the factors that are important to you. Shop around. Try to find a bank account that meets your needs.

In the UK, the Cooperative Bank, Triodos Bank and the Ecology Building Society are the leading ethical banks. The Charities Aid Foundation runs CafBank specially for charities.

Charitable status

If the work that your group is doing is charitable, you might wish to apply for charitable status. This will allow you to take advantage of a range of tax benefits and to receive grants from grant-making bodies which only give to charities.

To be a charity, you need to have a constitution which complies with the requirements of charity law. You may wish to take professional advice on drawing up a charitable constitution and on setting up as a charity.

For further information on how to become a charity and the benefits of charitable status, consult the Charity Commission (or the equivalent body in your own country). **www.charity-commission.gov.uk**

Some other issues to think about

There are all sorts of other matters you need to think about:

- **Data protection,** which limits the use you can make of your list of supporters.

- **Child protection,** which requires certain procedures and practices if you are working with children (under eighteen).

- **Equal opportunities,** both in the staff and volunteers you employ and in who has access to your services.

- **Public liability insurance,** if the work you are doing puts you at risk.

- **Inland Revenue requirements** for paying tax and National Insurance on the salaries you pay to your employees.

Getting Organized

115

10. KEEPING ACCOUNTS

You need to keep proper accounts so that you can be sure that you are spending your money properly and to be able to review your financial position from time to time.

A basic accounting system requires you to keep two sets of records:

1. Books of account: In a simple cashbook (obtainable from any office supplies shop) or using an Excel spreadsheet, you write down details of each item of income that you receive and each payment that you make. You will record the following details for each transaction:

the date of the receipt or payment;

a reference number;

the amount spent or received;

a description of the transaction;

a code which allocates the item to a particular income or expenditure category

2. Supporting documents for each transaction – for example, a till receipt, invoice or signed authorization form for each item of expenditure; or an attached explanatory letter or copy of an invoice you have issued for each item of income. These documents provide evidence that all the details of the transaction that you have recorded in your accounts are correct. You should put all the supporting documents in a file, writing a reference number on each which matches it to the entry in the cashbook.

For small organizations, this is all you need to do. Larger organizations may need to move to double entry bookkeeping and make adjustments to the *Receipts and Payments* accounts to produce *Income and Expenditure* accounts so that they more truly reflect the financial position. You will also at that stage probably want to use an accounting software package.

It is really important to keep you records up to date, writing the details of each new transaction in the cashbook as the income is received or payment made. This task is called "bookkeeping". You can easily do it yourself; or you may find some with experience of bookkeeping to help you.

Comparing actual and budgeted

In your budget you will have planned to spend so much on salaries, so much on running the office, so much on publicity, etc.

If you allocate each transaction to a particular category, this will help you to group similar

transactions together. For example, you will have a category for "Salaries". Adding up all the transactions which have been given allocated to the "Salaries" category will enable you to work out the total you have spent so far on salaries, and then to compare this with what you have budgeted for the year.

For each Committee Meeting, it is sensible to prepare a financial statement which shows the receipts and payments for the year so far as compared with the budget for the whole year. You can then easily see when income is not coming in as quickly as planned or expenditure is at a higher level than budgeted and needs to be better controlled if you are to avoid a financial crisis.

Here are some simple categories which you might use (adapt them so that they reflect the main items of income and expenditure that you are incurring):

Grants
Salaries
Donations
Volunteer expenses
Sales of publications
Office
Charges for services
Stationery and printing
Proceeds of fundraising event
Travel
Public collection
Programme costs
Sundry other costs

An asset register

You should also keep an asset register, which records details of every item of equipment that you have purchased, with the following details:

> **Date of purchase**
> **Cost**
> **Supplier**
> **Supplier's reference number**
> **Your reference number**

In a separate file, keep all receipts and copies of guarantees or warranties with your reference number clearly marked on each.

Further Information

Mango is a non-profit organization which provides financial services to charities. You can download the following from their website free of charge:

- Introduction to basic bookkeeping plus a basic bookkeeping example using Excel.

- What is double entry bookkeeping, an explanation.

- The Mango training manual and simple Excel financial system, which you can use for your accounting.

Getting Organized

117

11. COMMITTEES AND COMMITTEE MEETINGS

If you are establishing a formal organization, you will need to have a Management Committee of some sort. If you are an informal group, you may still want to have a group of people who will meet together from time to time to hear about progress and oversee the running of the project.

Forming a committee

Ideally, a committee should not be too large or too small. Between five and nine people will usually work well. Your constitution will set out how many people and how often they meet.

Everyone on the Committee should be committed to the group's mission and to its values. They may also bring different skills or different perspectives to the group. Some may be linked to other organizations with which you will have close dealings. Everyone is there to help make the venture a success.

From your committee members, you will need to select people to take on the following roles:

• **Chairperson,** to chair the meetings. This could be you, or it could be someone else. It could be the same person for each meeting. Or you might want to rotate the job.

• **Secretary,** to announce the meetings, and to record and circulate the Minutes.

• **Treasurer,** to oversee the finances, ensure that accounts are produced and present the financial reports.

You may also want other people on the committee to have a particular responsibility for:

• Public relations and publicity

• Fundraising

• Particular aspects of the project's work

How meetings should be run

- Circulate an agenda setting out the venue, start and finish times, and the business of the meeting.

- Circulate written reports in advance (wherever possible) for each agenda item, so that the Committee can think through things before the meeting.

- The person chairing the meeting should try to ensure that everyone has a say. Where there is no consensus, any reservations that people have should be noted.

- Once a decision is made, move on. Make the decision work. Don't continually go back to question whether it was the right decision.

- The meeting should be minuted, with action points clearly noted. This should show who is responsible for the particular action, and by when it should be completed.

- The Minutes should be agreed by the Chairperson, and then circulated as soon as possible after the meeting.

- Set the dates for future meetings well in advance. If some people find it hard to attend, they should be encouraged to resign.

- If you have the funds, offer to reimburse any reasonable expenses for attending (this could include childminding).

Items for your agenda

1. Apologies from those who are unable to attend.

2. Minutes of the last meeting, which should be run through to see that all actions have been followed up and to discuss any matters arising approved.

3. Committee membership, to discuss proposed new members or accept resignations.

4. Financial report, prepared by the Treasurer. At the final meeting for the year, a plan and a budget for the coming year should be prepared, discussed and agreed. At the meeting six months later, the accounts for the previous year will be approved.

5. Project report, to review progress and achievements.

6. Any other business, where any matters not covered elsewhere can be brought up.

7. Date of next meeting, to ensure that it's in people's diaries.

Getting Organized

119

GET THE MESSAGE OUT

Telling people about what you are doing is really important. It can give you feedback. It can get you supporters. It can help you mobilize resources.

Find audiences who will be interested in what you have to say, and offer to give a talk. Get on radio – mainstream national broadcasters or offbeat community radio stations – someone will be interested in giving you airtime. Get coverage in the press or write a letter to the editor. Create links between other people's websites and your own. Speak up at conferences – from the platform or from the floor. Participate in blogs and chatrooms and start to build a reputation for doing something.

Capture the essence of your message in a memorable phrase whether these are your own words or written for you by a speechwriter. Here are some examples of people who have done just that:

President John F. Kennedy, speaking at his inauguration on 20 January 1961, when power was passing to a new generation:

". . . my fellow Americans, ask not what your country can do for you; ask what you can do for your country. My fellow citizens of the world, ask not what America will do for you, but what together we can do for the freedom of man. Finally, whether you are citizens of America or citizens of the world, ask of us here the same high standards of strength and sacrifice which we ask of you. . . "

Jawaharlal Nehru, India's first Prime Minister, announcing the birth of a nation, India's independence on the night of 14 August 1947:

"At the stroke of the midnight hour, when the world sleeps, India will awake to life and freedom. A moment comes, which comes but rarely in history, when we step out from the old to the new, when an age ends, and when the soul of a nation, long suppressed, finds utterance . . . to the people of India, whose representatives we are, we make an appeal to join with us with faith and confidence in this great adventure."

Former US President **Bill Clinton** speaking at the UK Labour Party conference in September 2006, capturing the problems of the world in a simple paragraph:

". . . the modern interdependent world is unequal, unstable and unsustainable. It is unequal because of poverty, disease and the lack of access to education, capital and functioning government. It's unstable because of the threats of terror, weapons of mass destruction, failed states and the slaughter of innocents in places like Darfur. It's unsustainable because of climate change, oil and water depletion and environmental degradation."

SPEAK UP!
SPEAK OUT!

Sue Warner founded *SpeakersBank* to encourage people to speak up and speak out. Her own fear of standing up in public and speaking out was her starting point. This is what Sue has to say:

"Fear? No, make that abject terror. Until I was in my forties I lacked confidence and self-belief. I couldn't face an audience, however small without thinking people could see my heart beating. At work and at meetings I would often remain silent, even if I had a point of view.

"Then my sister encouraged me to visit a Toastmaster speaker club. I walked into a meeting in the late 1990s, and it changed my life. If anyone had told me that within two years I would be nominated the UK and Ireland Toastmaster of the Year, I'd have had them sedated or certified!

"I waited far too long to find out that I had a voice. Everyone has something to say. We all feel passionate about issues and causes but often fail to speak up and speak out when the opportunities arise. Since then I have focused all my time in developing public speaking training for those who least have a voice in today's society."

The *SpeakersBank* Speak Up! Speak Out! public speaking programme has now been delivered to over 20,000 people in schools and voluntary organizations in the UK

www.speakersbank.co.uk

HOW TO COMPLAIN

Complaining to whoever is responsible for the problem can be a good way of getting things changed. This is how Hilary Blume sets about it:

"How you complain matters. I always call the top person – the Company Chairman, the Leader of the Council or the Minister's office. You won't get though to them personally. But doing this means that your complaint will get passed to the right person with a note telling them to sort it out. Usually you will speak to a secretary. Take their name, and note the date and time. If nothing seems to happen, you can phone them again to remind them that the problem hasn't been dealt with.

"Start off by apologising for taking up their time. I ask them to be patient, as my explanation is likely to be long and involved. Usually they say that they will try, and then this makes it hard for them to cut me off in mid-stream.

"I often tell them how good their service usually is, and how disappointed I am that there has been a problem. I explain the problem. I try to get their sympathy, perhaps by saying something like this: 'Do you have children? I'm sure you know what it's like to wait three hours with a crying baby . . .' I then tell them what I want done. Behind what I say, there is an implication that I am determined, that I will take my complaint to a higher authority, go public, make a fuss at a public meeting – in essence, I will become more of a nuisance, if they don't give me a reasonable answer.

"Local and central government have official complaints procedures. These are designed to wear you down. They may involve you writing a letter which will get a standard (and often irrelevant) reply, or they will refer you to a call centre, where the staff have no power to deal with anything. Just tell them that this is not satisfactory, and that you propose to proceed to the next stage. There are about five levels for local complaints, the final being the Ombudsman. In practice by Level 2 – a response by the Chief Executive – your complaint will probably have been deal with.

"Remember, complaining makes the world better for everyone. Do it. Articulate people need to speak up to redress wrongs. But at the same time, remember to give praise when it's due. I set aside around an hour a day for doing all of this."

Key points:

- Complain only about the things that can be changed.

- Make sure that you do it effectively.

- Deal with the person who can put things right. You must find out who that person is.

- Know what you want. This might be compensation, an apology, or a change to the procedures.

- Have the evidence to back up your complaint.

- Start off by being hurt and upset. Be polite. Never lose your temper.

- Imply that there will be a lot of trouble if you don't get satisfaction, that you are persistent, and that you have power and contacts.

- Don't give up.

- Get publicity for what you are doing, if you think this will help.

Hilary Blume is Director of the Charities Advisory Trust, and creator of Peace Oil *(page 78)*

The Complaints Choir

Tellervo Kalleinen and Oliver Kochta-Kalleinen were out walking in Helsinki. They were discussing how to channel the energy that people put into complaining into something productive. There is a Finnish expression "Valituskuoro", meaning "Complaints Choir", which is used for lots of people complaining simultaneously. A thought occurred: "Why don't we take this expression literally and organize a real Complaints Choir?"

Birmingham in England seemed a perfect place. Fifteen participants were found by distributing flyers and posters. Local musician Mike Hurley turned their complaints into an easy-to-learn song. There were two weeks of rehearsals, and then the performance itself. *"I want my money back..."* became a hit.

Since then, Kalleinen and Kochta-Kalleinen have organized events in Helsinki, St Petersburg and Hamburg.

The complaints vary from small daily irritations to global issues. In Birmingham, people complained about unfriendly bus drivers, bad bananas and slow computers. In Helsinki, it was of mobile phone ring tones, people on public transport who smell and the fact that Finland always loses to Sweden in competitions. In Hamburg, the complaints were more political, and in St Petersburg the emphasis was on the existential!

The website encourages people all over the world to form their own Complaints Choirs and to submit video documentation, photos, descriptions and comment. Word is spreading. People have organized choirs in Bodö, Philadelphia, Toronto, and Israel. An International Autistic Complaints Choir is also being planned.

www.complaintschoir.org and
www.ykon.org/kochta-kalleinen

A BLOGGER'S TALE

I kept my promise to those who died: It is 12:23 am, in the early morning of 4 June 2005. Today is the sixteenth anniversary of the Tiananmen Square Massacre in Beijing. When the event happened in 1989, I was sitting in a tunnel outside the Xinhua News Agency office in Hong Kong where hunger strikers had set up. We were supporting the students in China. We wanted democracy for them and for ourselves. We no longer wanted to be colonial subjects of Britain, and we did not want to be subjects of the Communist Party either. We wanted to be free.

About two, maybe three hours later, I heard the first shots coming through the radio, followed by the sound of singing, screaming and tanks reverberating though the walls. We looked at each other and saw tears streaming down our faces.

We all know now that China will use tanks against those who seek democracy, but until then we did not. I think it was at that moment that *Glutter* was born in my head, when I heard the ending of the 1989 Democratic Movement on the radio, in a tunnel with bright fluorescent lights. I was fifteen.

If not at that moment, it was soon afterwards. I would make a promise that only young women with no experience in the world could make

with as little doubt as I did: *I will not forget. I promise to remember forever. I will live my life better and for all of us because I am alive and you are no longer. I won't let this happen again. I will remind the world for you, the students of Tiananmen Square. My Heroes. My Big Brothers and Sisters.*

I made those promises in haste, in fear, in naivety. It never occurred to me how something like this could be achieved, or if it was even possible. I only knew that it sounded right, and all the adults were yelling those things out of loudspeakers.It is only tonight that I'm thinking that all this writing, all the photos and artwork I have done in the name of democracy, the cyber-protest I organized, the interviews I agreed to, and the stories I published in the name of free speech are not only because I fervently believe in it, but also because *blogging allows me to keep my promises to the dead.*

I think people should know that this is why I have managed to create **Glutter.** Not because I followed any rules, or copied anybody else. Not because I wanted attention or wanted to make a name. I often prefer it best when it is quiet, and I will let the blog die a little when I feel there is too much attention focused on it. Because then I can just write what I want, and tell the story that needs to be told in the way I like without any pressure.

My advice to those interested in starting a blog is:

• Don't listen to anyone except yourself.

• Don't read anyone else's blog and try to emulate it.

• Don't sit down with a list of "musts" and try to achieve it.

I broke so many rules because I didn't know there were any. And I did just fine.

All you need to create a blog is the will to get started. All you need to keep one going is a will to record what you have to say. I hope you can convey enough of your own convictions to inspire others to fight for change. That's the wisdom I want to impart.

It is now 2:33am. I can hear gunshots. Put! Put! Put! I hear them every year at this time. I was fifteen, probably too young to have experienced the events the way I did. But others were too young to die.

Yan Sham-Shackleton's blog talks about art as well as politics. Her outspokenness and pro-democracy stance in Hong Kong mean that she is regularly censored inside China. Her blog, Glutter, was nominated by Reporters Without Borders for a free speech award.

Glutter is a mixture of "Glitter" and "Gutter":

www.glutter.org

The Handbook for Bloggers and Cyber-Dissidents tells you all you need to know about blogging. Download it from the Reporters Without Borders website:

www.rsf.org

Find out about podcasting from *Podcast Solutions: a complete guide to podcasting* by Michael Geoghehan and Dan Klass, which comes complete with sample programmes for your computer.

125

ACTION GUIDE: COMMUNICATION

1. GETTING YOUR MESSAGE OUT

If you want to create real change, it helps to have the "oxygen of publicity". Getting publicity should not be an ego trip for you. Your aim should be to publicise your cause, to get your ideas into the public arena, and to build your credibility, which will help you with both your lobbying and your fundraising.

Don't wait for reporters to telephone you asking for an interview or a story. They won't and you won't get heard. You have to contact them and persuade them to give you coverage; and you should also think up creative ways of getting yourself noticed.

Take a look at these ideas. If you think that any might help you get your message out, then do them.

Action Guide

Creating awareness

1. Distribute wristbands, ribbons and button badges

Get people to wear these to show solidarity and spread awareness. Red ribbons for HIV/AIDS, pink for breast cancer, each cause has its own colour. What's yours?

2. Create a catchy slogan

Put what you need to say in just a few words, then print your slogan on banners, placards or even bumper stickers.

3. Flypost a poster, hand out handbills, stick up stickers

Do this to publicize your cause or promote an event.

4. Put it on a T-shirt

. . . and show people you care. You can do it yourself, using volunteers. Or there are websites that will do the design and printing for you.

5. Display your message in an unusual place

Write it on a banknote, embroider it on the back of your rucksack, write it in lights in your window . . .

Mobilizing people power

1. Organize a demonstration or a march

Sit down, stand up or go for a walk. Mobilize lots of people and show the strength of opinion. This will put pressure on decision-makers.

2. Organize a petition

. . . and then get lots and lots of people to sign it. You can now do this online at the Petition Site.

3. Meet up and act together

More people doing things together become much more powerful than doing it alone. Why not find or start a local MeetUp or Green Drinks group.

4. SMS a call to action

. . . or podcast your latest news; Hrnss nw tchnlgy to help promote your cause.

5. Get people to pledge

Ask them to commit to do something. *PledgeBank* helps you multiply your impact. Getting forty-nine other people to do the same as you will make fifty times the difference.

Doing it virtually

1. Create your own website

First get yourself a memorable URL. Then get someone to design it. And finally get lots of people to visit it. Give them something to do. Ask them to give you their email address.

2. Send out a regular e-newsletter

Collect email addresses from everyone you meet and anyone who is interested. A large emailing list will enable you to circulate a newsletter widely at very little cost.

3. Become a blogger

Provide your readers with information, analysis, ideas, sources and resources. Make your blog the blog of choice for anyone interested in the cause you are addressing.

4. Spread the word by viral marketing

Create intriguing messages that people will forward to their friends. If enough recipients send the message on, then it will start to spread around the world.

5. Lulu your book at little cost

Use the lulu.com website to publish your book and have it printed on demand. This low-cost method enables you to produce books for a tiny readership as well as publish best-sellers.

Getting media coverage

1. Speak up and speak out

Do this anywhere and everywhere. At Speakers Corner, during question time at conferences and meetings, and even by talking to the person behind you in the supermarket checkout queue.

2. Get it into the newspapers

Get your story into the mainstream and the alternative press. A news item, a feature, a reader's letter, a photo with a caption.

3. Make a video

. . . and then find ways of showing it. Put it on YouTube, stream it from your website, show it at meetings.

4. Organize a stunt

Do something that will attract a lot of media attention. Friends of the Earth got started in the UK by returning thousands of non-returnable bottles to Schweppes and piling them up outside the company's HQ in London.

5. Phone in to chat shows

If nobody is asking you to speak, then try telephoning into a chat show to get your voice heard. There may be someone amongst the audience who will be interested in what you have to say.

Communication

127

Lobbying for change

1. Experience the problem
Go out in a wheelchair for a day, eat in the dark, do a homeless sleep out. Persuade others to join you. Then think about what it would be like to experience the problem all the time.

2. Publicize the facts
Become the expert. Find out as much as you can. Then use the facts to make a compelling case.

3. Lobby your elected representatives
They *are* there to represent you. Make them work for their living.

4. Act against companies
Buy one share, and make your point at shareholder meetings. And use your power as a consumer to make positive choices about what to buy as well as boycotting the bad.

5. Get people to put their money where their mouth is
Create some easy ways for people to give to you. Suggest some simple fundraising ideas for them to raise money from their friends.

Doing something unusual

1. Bare all for your beliefs
Strip off and spell out your message with naked bodies. You will attract media attention as you make your point

2. Become a biotic baker and "pie" someone
Combat pomposity and indifference with a dash of humour. But choose your victims with care. They will not be pleased. The Biotic Baking Brigade will show you how.

3. Withhold sex
This technique has been used successfully by rural women in Turkey, peace activists in Sudan and by Lysistrata-lovers all over the world.

4. Organize a Flashmob or create a Critical Mass
These are spontaneous gatherings in public places, which can make a splash. Use these techniques to reclaim streets and public spaces for people and to have a bit of fun.

5. Become a guerrilla advertiser
Use your creativity to get your message noticed. Paint graffiti in detergent on dirty walls, designate a smoking area on the pavement outside your office with anti-smoking messages and an ashtray . . .

JOIN THE BUY NOTHING DAY PARADE

Come "Traffic Jamming" with the Stop Shopping Gospel Choir and the Not Buying It Band. Bring your own music, wear bright colours. Wear red; at least wear a Santa hat. This year we are Buying Nothing For Global Cooling.

Traffic Jamming is defined as *"That direct action in which citizens step into a roadway where cars and trucks are stopped, then preach and sing to the motorists while offering them information about global warming and how it's caused by buying and driving cars."*

REV BILLY AND THE CHURCH OF STOP SHOPPING:

http://ReverendBilly.org

JOIN THE STOP GLOBAL WARMING VIRTUAL MARCH

Submit your email and join the global movement to get something done.

"There is no more important cause than the call to action to save our planet. This is a movement about change, as individuals, as a country (the USA), and as a global community. We are all contributors to global warming and we all need to be part of the solution. Join our 518,049 supporters and become part of the movement to demand solutions to global warming now."

www.stopglobalwarming.org

Bare Witness: **www.barewitness.org** and **www.baringwitness.org**

Biotic Baking Brigade: **www.bioticbakingbrigade.org**

Blogger: **www.blogspot.com**

Green Drinks: **www.greendrinks.org**

Publish it on LuLu: **www.lulu.com**

MeetUp: **www.meetup.com**

Petition Site: **www.thepetitionsite.com** and **www.petitiononline.com**

PledgeBank: **www.pledgebank.com**

T-shirt sites: **www.cafepress.com** and **www.comboutique.com**

YouTube: **www.youtube.com**

2.
USING CASE STUDIES

Tell a human story, don't just explain your cause in abstract terms or rattle off a lot of facts and figures.

People will understand the issue better if they can see how it affects one person or one community. And they may be moved enough by what you tell them to do something – to take action, give money, sign a petition, volunteer their time.

This is how you might describe the general problem of child labour . . .

According to Save the Children: Millions of children around the world have to work to support themselves and their families. Many do light or part-time work that can be fitted in around school. But many others are involved in dangerous or exploitative labour that harms their development, wrecks their health and denies them an education.

This is how you might show how its affects children . . .

The story of Sankar: The railway stations in India are home for thousands of children. Some have left their homes in villages outside the city. Other children come from poverty-stricken homes nearby. Sankar, for instance, lives nearby but in an unstable home. His father is no longer part of the family. His mother is seldom home. Sankar sells bottled water to train passengers at Bhubaneswar railway station, in order to earn enough to survive. On average, a child will make 50 to 100 Rupees (about $2-$3) a day doing this, which will pay for food and other bare essentials. Sankar and the other children bed down wherever they can in the station – on the floor, on benches, on piles of luggage.

Scavenging in Phnom Penh: To find the main dump for Cambodia's capital, drive down the dirt road near the radio station in the commune of Stung Meanchey. Three siblings – the elder boys Kayrith (14) and Ratha (12) and their younger sister Minea (10) – work there as scavengers. The children live near the dump with their father Bo, mother Sam On, younger sisters Srey Yaan (5) and Srey Yan (4) and ten-month-old baby brother Sam Naang. Their home is a typical two-storey, bamboo-framed shack with a corrugated tin roof, walls patched together from scavenged materials. The children sleep together on the top level, where the floor is made of slatted bamboo. The parents sleep on the damp and muddy ground floor, so that they can guard the flock of ducks they scoot into a pen beside the cooking platform. It's dangerous living there. One day, their cousin, Thavara, sank in the garbage up to her neck. And to reduce the stench, scavengers set the rubbish on fire so it smoulders all the time, emitting noxious fumes and causing respiratory problems.

These stories are from the Child Labor Photo Project, organized by the Tides Center, which also documents the problem in pictures:

www.childlaborphotoproject.org

PhotoVoice goes one step further and gives children cameras so that they can document their own lives. Visit their online gallery at:

www.photovoice.org

Some guidelines for writing case studies

- **Talk to people:** Find out their stories. Ask them about their problems, what is being done about them, their ideas for how things could be better. Then write it down . . .

- **Make people excited:** Explain the story in a conversational way. Imagine yourself talking to someone at a party with real enthusiasm about this one person. That's how you should be telling your story.

- **Don't be long-winded:** Keep it short and to the point. Anything between 50–200 words should be quite sufficient.

- Grab the reader's attention by giving your case study **a catchy headline.**

- If you can, **include a good photograph** or a video clip.

3. PRODUCING LEAFLETS AND POSTERS

To get your message out, you will need clearly written and nicely designed printed materials . . . which don't cost a fortune to produce.

You might need the following:

- A simple **leaflet** explaining what you are doing and suggesting ways in which people can help you.

- A small **poster** to put up on noticeboards asking people to contact you if they want more information or would like to get involved.

- A **fact sheet** giving basic information and statistics about the issue.

You may also want to produce stickers, bumper stickers, postcards, business cards and other printed matter to help spread the message.

And as you get established, you will need a more detailed annual report which reviews your work and shows how you have spent your money.

Prepare a leaflet explaining your work

Use a simple leaflet to explain your work and encourage people to support you. Make sure that you include "a call to action", asking people to do something specific. And don't forget to include a reply address and a telephone number for those wanting further information. Produce this in an electronic version as well as a printed version.

But producing a leaflet is only half the process. You also need to get it widely circulated. To get the message out, you can:

- Send a copy to *everyone on your mailing list*.

- Give copies to *colleagues, volunteers and well-wishers* to hand out at meetings and conferences and to give to anyone they meet who expresses an interest.

- Have copies in your office or at home to give out to visitors.

- Include a copy with *every letter you send out*.

Try to think of some other ways of reaching out. For example, you could ask your local newsagent to circulate your leaflet with newspaper deliveries, or you could post them yourself through letterboxes in your neighbourhood.

The components of a successful leaflet

A 4-page A5 leaflet is a cheap and effective format – and this could be printed in full colour, or in black and one other colour, or in just a single colour.

Here is a suggested structure for a simple leaflet:

Page 1

The **name** of your project, a **logo** and a **strapline**.

A **photograph** and a **headline** plus about forty words of explanation showing how you are helping one person.

Page 2

A brief **background** to what you have done and why you are doing it (a headline plus about 100 words).

A table showing three **key achievements** (or your aims, if you are just starting).

A **quotation** or **endorsement** from someone important.

A **photograph** and **caption** (of about six words) illustrating the problem.

Page 3

A **case study** (a headline plus about fifty words).

An **explanation of the need** (a headline plus about eighty words) plus three key facts or figures.

A **photograph** and caption illustrating what you are doing to solve the problem.

Page 4

Your **plans for the future** (a headline plus about sixty words).

A **call to action**: how people can help you (list of three different things that people can do).

A **reply address** and a telephone number for further information.

A **website address**.

Your leaflet should be well planned. It could have a theme running through it (for example, "*Helping people to help themselves*" or "*Making waves in Brighton*").

Some things to avoid in your leaflet

- Don't be boring. You want people to pick up your leaflet and read it.

- Include only information which will be of interest.

- Don't use generalizations. Give facts and examples.

- Don't produce a leaflet that is poorly designed and badly printed. This suggests incompetence. And don't print your leaflet on expensive paper or thick card. This suggests that you waste your resources.

4. CREATING YOUR OWN WEBSITE

Your website may the first place people will go to when they want to find out more about you. So you need one, and it needs to be good.

Step 1. Decide why you want to have your own website

Who do you want to reach? What do you want to tell them? What do you want them to do?

You can use your website to:

• Provide **information** about your cause, your work, your organization.

• Publish **news, ideas and thoughts** (via a blog).

• Provide access to **resources** – including tools for taking action, reports, photographs, audio and video clips

• Provide **fun and games** and engage people with your cause

• Enable the **sharing of information** and ideas through forums and chat rooms

• **Sell books and merchandise online**, directly or through affiliate programmes.

• **Raise money** for your work by getting advertising and sponsorship

• **Encourage action,** by suggesting things for people to do to address the problem.

Step 2. Register a domain name

Your domain name (known as a URL) is important. It should be easy to remember, easy to type, and readily identifiable with your organization. What would be the best name for you? You may find that what you want is not available. Someone may have already registered it – and even if they are not using it, they may not be prepared to sell it to you at a price you can afford.

Your domain name will include an "extension" which is in two parts. The first part reflects the sort of organization you are: .com .co .biz (for businesses) .org .net .coop .info .museum .edu (for different types of non-profit organization).

Your extension may also include a country indicator. This is optional, as you may find a suitable domain name without this, which will give a more international feel. You may want to use your own country indicator to show where you are based – for example .uk (UK), .fr (France), etc. But also think about using these: .tv (Tuvalu) where part of the registration fee goes to a small country threatened by global warming and .it (Italy) where the "it" can become part of a slogan that your domain name spells out.

You might want to register a range of URLs, such as .org .net .com .org.uk so that if someone types in a variant of the name you want to use they will arrive at your own website.

Step 3. Plan the structure and content of your website

You will organize your content into a number of different pages, so you need to plan how the pages link together. Make your website as easy to navigate as possible. Think about where your visitors will want to go to, and make it easy for them to get there. A good starting point is to look at other people's websites, and to see what you like and dislike about them, and then design yours to incorporate the best features and avoid the worst.

Step 4. Create the pages

This involves writing the text (not too many words) and gathering together the images you want to use. You will then work with a website designer to design the pages and incorporate the features you require (such as a blog or a chatroom or online giving). If you have the skills or are prepared to teach yourself, you can do this yourself.

Step 5. Find a host

Your website needs hosting on a web server. There are many companies providing this service. The cost will depend on the features offered and the amount of space you need. Webhosting is not expensive. Ask around to see which hosts other people are using, how much they are paying and whether they are satisfied.

Step 6. Encourage people to visit your website

How are you going to market your website? How are you going to increase the number of people visiting your website? There's no point putting a lot of effort into creating a great website if nobody ever visits it!

Step 7. Keep your website up to date

Setting up a website is only the beginning. You need to keep it up to date. You may want to continually refresh the information so that people visiting it again and again find things of interest that were not there before. This all take times, and possibly money. Allow for this in your planning.

If you still don't know what to do, then take a look at:

www.havingmyownwebsite.net and
www.virtuallyignorant.com

5. WRITING LETTERS

Letters can make a difference. They can change somebody's view. They can persuade them to do something. We've almost stopped writing letters. We send emails instead. But finding an email in your in-box is not quite the same as getting a letter through the post.

So send a letter asking someone to do something.

Write to all your friends, telling them about what you are planning to do to save the world. Invite them to join you or support you.

Write and complain next time something goes wrong.

Write a letter to the editor of your local newspaper, adding to the debate, pointing out a new fact about a recently reported issue, or raising a completely new issue that the readers might be interested in.

Write to your elected representative. They often refer to "their postbag" which they see as a barometer of public opinion. Your letter could seriously influence their thinking on an issue.

Write to the Prime Minister. Tell him what you think about a nuclear future – if you want the government to change its policies on nuclear power and nuclear weapons.

Write to them

Go to **writetothem.com**, which will tell you who your Member of Parliament, or Member of the European Parliament, or Local Councillor is. You can then send them a fax or an email. Just insert your postcode and write the letter you want. It's sent automatically. If you live outside the UK, then you'll have to do your own research to find out who to write to and how to contact them.

You can also send a letter to a Lord. Lords do not represent a constituency as MPs do. So you will need to think about which Lord to write to. Using the writetothem.com website, you can send your letter to:

- A Lord who is interested in your topic (as indicated by recent parliamentary debates).

- A Lord who has some association with your place of residence.

- A Lord who shares your birthday.

- A random Lord. You have no idea who to write to; the website suggests someone.

www.writetothem.com

Start a chain letter by email

Dear friends who care about our earth. Judge for yourself if you want to take action.

In the Valle de San Felix, the purest water in Chile runs from two rivers, fed by two glaciers. Water is a most precious resource, and wars will be fought for it. Indigenous farmers use the water; there is no unemployment, and they provide the second largest source of income for the area.

Under the glaciers has been found a huge deposit of gold, silver and other minerals. To get at these, it would be necessary to break, to destroy the glaciers – something never conceived of in the history of the world – and to make two huge holes, each as big as a whole mountain, one for extraction and one for the mine's rubbish tip.

The project is called Pascua Lama. The company is called Barrick Gold. The operation is planned by a multinational company, one of whose members is George Bush Senior. The Chilean Government approved the project to start in 2006.

The only reason it hasn't started yet is because the farmers have got a temporary stay of execution. If they destroy the glaciers, they will not just destroy the source of especially pure water, but they will permanently contaminate the two rivers so they will never again be fit for human or animal consumption because of the use of cyanide and sulphuric acid in the extraction process. Every last gram of gold will go abroad to the multinational company and not one will be left with the people whose land it is. They will only be left with the poisoned water and the resulting illnesses.*

We ask you to circulate this message amongst your friends in the following way. Please copy this text, paste it into a new email adding your signature and send it to everyone in your address book. Please, will the hundredth person to receive and sign the petition, send it to noapascualama@yahoo.ca to be forwarded to the Chilean Government.

No to Pascua Lama Open-cast mine in the Andean Cordillera on the Chilean-Argentine frontier. We ask the Chilean Government not to authorize the Pascua Lama project to protect the whole of three glaciers, the purity of the water of the San Felix Valley and El Transito, the quality of the agricultural land of the region of Atacama, the quality of life of the Diaguita people and of the whole population of the region.

There are then numbered spaces for 100 signatures, which are filled in as the petition is sent from one person to the next until all 100 signatures have been obtained. Any petition about an issue of global importance will soon spread around the world!

6. ORGANIZING A DEMO

Demos are a great way of demonstrating the strength of public opinion, both to the people you want to influence and to the public at large.

If you do decide to organize a demo, make sure it is successful.

These are some of the things you will need:

1. A clear objective. Ask yourself what you want to achieve. But try also to be realistic – ask yourself what it is possible to achieve. Make your objective as specific as you can; don't be woolly.

2. A communication network, to report on what you have done. The media are your allies in getting you publicity. Make your demo as newsworthy and as photogenic as you can. Try to get the maximum amount of coverage.

3. People. Numbers *are* important. Involve as many people as you can. Recruit lots more supporters at your demo. Ask people for their contact details. Grow your network. Develop coalitions with other like-minded groups. And then mobilize this support when you need to.

4. Expertise. Identify and get the support of experts and celebrities who are prepared to speak up for you. They will lend authority to your cause.

5. Legal advice. Lawyers can tell you how far you can go without getting locked up. This is important for any direct action.

6. Knowledge of your enemy. See what resources they have at their disposal, and what their weaknesses are. Think about where and how you can best apply pressure. Know their arguments better than they do. Provoke a reaction, which you then go on to use for your benefit.

7. Get the sympathy of the public. Keep the public on your side. Appeal to their sense of fairness. Take care not to confuse your message with party politics or sectarian viewpoints.

Some practical advice

Arrive with banners and placards: Create slogans which are catchy, but at the same time convey the injustice of the situation and present your alternative. Press coverage of these will get your message out to millions. Give out leaflets explaining your case to passers-by.

Have designated spokespeople: You need to ensure that whoever speaks is "on message". Direct the media to these people.

Present your demands, both publicly in speeches at the demonstration and when you meet the authorities. Give them a specific time in which to meet your demands.

Make it clear that in the event of your demands not being met, then you will be back, to protest again and more vocally.

End in triumph with everyone present believing that you are firmly on the way to success.

Some rules for radicals

Saul Alinsky is a "guru of community organizing". In his book *Rules for Radicals* (1971) he defined tactics as *"doing what you can with what you've got"*. He listed a set of rules for success, including:

1. Power is what you have, but it is also what "the enemy" thinks you have. So always give the impression that your point of view is backed by large numbers of people (even when this is not yet the case) and that they feel threatened by it.

2. Make the enemy live up to their own book of rules. If they break their own rules, then discredit and embarrass them. Use public ridicule; it is an extremely potent weapon.

3. If the action drags on too long, it will become a drag. Set a timescale for achieving success. And keep up the pressure. Focus all of your energy on achieving your desired outcome.

4. Pick your target. Your target should be a specific person, not an intangible institution. Make that person the object of your attack.

5. Make them feel threatened by you. You need to articulate a threat – of what will happen if your demands are not met. You need to appear well-enough organized to be able to carry out that threat.

6. Always have a realistic alternative, which you can present to them and to the public at large. Never miss an opportunity to communicate this.

7. Believe that you are in the right: there may be arguments on both sides, and you may need to compromise in the end to reach a positive outcome. But you must believe that you are right. Polarize the argument – you are absolutely right, they are absolutely wrong – then act with conviction.

Contributed by Alistair McConnachie

Alistair McConnachie is the director of Sovereignty, an advocacy group which campaigns for popular democracy, not plutocracy; economic democracy, not debt slavery; localization, not globalization; energy independence, not dependence; and food sovereignty, not food poverty. **www.sovereignty.org.uk**

Communication

139

7.
ORGANIZING A PETITION

An effective way of gathering support for an issue is to start a petition.

The days of knocking on doors in a residential neighbourhood begging for people's signatures have long passed, except if you are organizing a neighbourhood campaign – when everyone you ask will be interested, either for or against.

The Internet has created a fast and easy mechanism for collecting thousands and even millions of signatures.

Your petition which you are asking people to sign up to should:

- **Explain the issue,** which you are asking people to sign up to.

- **Give some concrete facts,** which encapsulate the importance of the issue in a nutshell.

- **Be brief** – not more than half a page. People won't read more.

Create your petition online. These two websites enable you to set up and distribute your petition. It's all completely free.

The Petition Site:
www.thepetitionsite.com/create.html
PetitionOnline:
www.petitiononline.com/petition.html

Don't just post your petition, hoping that visitors to the site will sign up to it. A few people will. But you need to put some real effort into encouraging people to visit your online petition and sign it. Set yourself a target for the number of signatures you will get. Then email everyone you know asking them to sign your petition and to tell lots of other people to do the same.

After you have collected all the signatures, you need to do something with it. Send it to politicians, companies, and leaders – whoever can help you work toward getting the change you want. Get publicity for it in the press. If you've collected a lot of signatures, it's news!

The Hobbit Petition: save the Middle Earth!

How to collect more signatures than you ever dreamed possible:

- Send emails to your friends asking them to sign the petition.

- Post links on relevant discussion boards. This is often an excellent way of quickly reaching lots of interested people.

- Contact writers and journalists who write about the topic and tell them about your petition.

- Send out a press release announcing your petition (this can be particularly effective once you've collected quite a lot of signatures).

- Talk about your petition in online chat rooms.

- Add a link to your petition in your email signature.

- Add links to your petition on your website.

- Ask special interest groups with large audiences to add a link on their website or in their newsletters.

- Submit your petition page to search engines (it usually takes between three and four weeks to be indexed). Type into Google *"submit search engines"* to find a way of reaching a lot of search engines for free.

We, the undersigned, wish to make clear our strong desire to see a quality film adaptation of J. R. R. Tolkien's The Hobbit. *Having spent the last three years in Middle- earth, under the spell of magician Peter Jackson and the wizards of Weta Workshop, we find ourselves only wanting more. The Tale of the Ring is incomplete without the story of its finding by Bilbo, and the other aspects of his adventure make for a captivating cinematic journey as well.*

Fans know that the film rights reside with New Line, while distribution is the legal domain of MGM/United Artists. It would be heartbreaking for the fans to be denied this film, simply because of this rift in rights. Surely an agreement can be reached that will prove mutually advantageous to the studios. The phenomenal success of The Lord of the Rings trilogy clearly demonstrates that there is a huge fan base worldwide, ready to support The Hobbit *in like manner.*

Please work together to eliminate this barrier to the film's making and distribution. We, the fans, will make it worth your while. We are not ready to leave Middle-earth!

In addition to showing support for this project by signing this petition, fans can make their wishes known by writing a tactful, concise letter to the following persons (addresses given):
Robert K Shaye, New Line Cinema Corporation
Alex Yemenidjian, Metro-Goldwyn-Mayer Inc.
Danny Rosett, United Artists Corporation

By December 2006, over 55,000 people had signed this petition.

8.
GETTING MEDIA COVERAGE

There are a wide range of media which might be interested in covering your story.

They include:

- Broadcast television, including daytime TV and news channels.
- National and local radio (local radio can be especially important).
- Community radio.
- National newspapers.
- Local newspapers and freesheets.
- Magazines, journals and newsletters.
- Electronic newsletters and news services, including blogs.

The press coverage you might try to get includes:

- A **news story** covering something newsworthy that you are doing.
- A **feature article** on the issue, your campaign and the human stories of the people involved.
- A **photograph** with a caption.
- A **listing in** a "Forthcoming Events" or "Useful Services" column.
- A **letter** to the editor, which you write and send to them with your point of view.

Local radio coverage could include:

- A local **news story.**
- An **interview** or a more informal chat.
- A **feature** about the issue you are tackling, which includes something about your project.
- An **announcement** of an event you are organizing.
- Your contribution to a **phone-in** discussion.

Making the news: ten tips for getting coverage

There are all sorts of opportunities for getting media coverage, which people often fail to take advantage of. For example, you could:

1. Celebrate a **milestone:** your 100th supporter or the first £1,000 raised or a major grant or sponsorship.

2. Report an important **new development** in your campaign.

3. Announce your **future plans.**

4. Make a **prediction** or a forecast, especially if it is controversial.

5. Launch the publication of a **report** into the issue which includes what you have discovered through your work or the results of a survey.

6. Circulate your latest **newsletter** which contains news and views, and include a letter or press release highlighting some important or interesting information that it contains.

7. Get coverage for **events or activities** that you are running. You can try to get advance publicity as well as on-the-day coverage of your event.

8. Organize a **stunt,** where something very unusual will happen, which you have designed especially to get as much publicity as you can.

9. Issue a **call to action** – especially if the issue is topical (such as an important new government report on global warming) and where society is looking for some answers.

10. Do anything with **a celebrity.** The right celebrity for your organization will make getting publicity far easier.

Dealing with journalists

It can be really helpful if you get to know journalists who might be interested in writing about you. Some will be on the staff of the newspaper, some will be freelance. Try to identify a few journalists to approach and think how you might meet them. Try to develop a friendly relationship with them (perhaps occasionally meeting for a chat). Then when they need someone to comment on a particular issue, they will naturally turn to you. And when you have a really good story, you can alert them or even give them "an exclusive".

Press releases

One important way of getting media coverage is to issue a press release whenever there is something newsworthy. This will provide a journalist with all the information they need to decide whether to cover the story and a contact number for finding out more.

Journalists get tens of press releases every day. There is a recognized format for producing them; but yours has to stand out from the crowd and grab the journalist's attention.

Ten tips for writing a press release:

1. Give the press release a **title**, which says exactly what it's about, and a **date,** which shows when it was issued.

2. Write in **plain English**: use short words and sentences and no jargon.

3. **Double space** it and have wide margins. This makes it more readable.

4. Keep it as **short** as you can. One page, if you can manage it; two pages maximum.

5. If longer than one page, **staple the pages** together, to ensure that the journalist reads everything.

6. Use your press release to **highlight something newsworthy** which will be of interest to readers.

7. Set out **your viewpoint,** and explain why it is of interest. Additional facts can be included at the bottom as "Notes for Editors".

8. Include a **quotation,** as this can then be printed in the article as quote, just as if the person had been interviewed.

9. Give a **contact name** and phone number, so they can get in touch with you if they need more information. Make sure someone is available on that number.

10. Put an **embargo** on publication until a specified date and time, which will reassure editors that the story will not break before then. You can set an embargo date and time to coincide with light news periods (when there is a greater chance of getting coverage) or for a particular programme or publication (like a lunchtime chat show or evening edition of the local paper) where you are hoping to get coverage.

Photographs:

If there is something very visual, you can send out a photograph with your press release. If you do this, write a caption on the reverse. This will highlight the key point made by the photograph, and they could simply lift this and use it as their own caption if they decide to publish the photo. Alternatively, you could try inviting the local newspaper to send a photographer.

Press conferences:

If you have something really important to announce or if you have a celebrity speak on your behalf, then you might want to call a press conference – where you invite members of the press and broadcast media to come and hear your news. If there is a strong visual element, you could organize a photocall, where they send a photographer as well as a journalist. But what you are doing has to be really important to make journalists want to come along.

THE EVERYDAY ACTIVIST

Everything You Need to Know to Get
Off Your Backside and Make a Difference

by Michael Norton

Published by Boxtree on 19th October 2007; priced £9.99

THE ESSENTIAL GUIDE TO AN ETHICAL LIFESTYLE

There is huge debate about whose responsibility it is to change the world. From politicians and celebrities to ordinary people like you and I, everyone is being held to account for their personal impact on our planet. *The Everyday Activist* offers the solution. Packed with inspirational stories, fresh ideas and easy-to-follow, practical advice, this inspirational book is a must-have guide for anyone who wants to make a difference.

MICHAEL NORTON has changed the face of social innovation in Great Britain. Over the past thirty years, Michael has created several highly successful socially progressive programmes, which have affected thousands of lives all over the country.

Visit his website www.365act.com and blogspot www.365ways.blogspot. com to find out more about his projects.

Notes to editors:
- Extremely topical, particularly in the aftermath of Live Earth.
- Michael's last book, *365 Ways to Change the World,* has received huge critical acclaim and become a word-of-mouth bestseller.

Praise for 365 Ways to Change the World:

'Michael Norton is a one-man ideas factory' Guardian

'An enticing and informative book . . . I finally stopped being a cynic'
Daily Mail

- Michael Norton is available for interview and to write features. For further information, please contact Sandra Taylor; s.taylor@macmillan.co.uk or 020 7014 6093

Communication

145

GET THE MONEY

You will almost always need some money to turn your ideas into action – money for your project costs, for incidental expenditure such as travel, for publicity and promotion . . . Then there are the costs of setting up an organization, preparing annual accounts, etc.

You might be able to pay all these costs out of your own pocket. Or you could persuade a group of friends to back you, each contributing a small proportion of what you need. Or you might organize a fundraising event. Or you might look for a grant.*

When you are starting out, you may have a regular job that brings in the money to pay your rent, eat and generally enjoy yourself. As your project develops, you might find that you are having to devote more and more time to it. At that stage you will need to decide if you want to make your efforts to change the world a full-time career. Remember though, that if you do this, you will need to raise money to pay yourself a salary.

One problem is that it is easier to raise money once you and your work get known about and you have achieved some success. It is far harder to get funded when you are an unknown just starting out. But you don't let this deter you! Funders are looking for great projects to support, and success in fundraising is all about asking effectively and being persistent.

One idea is to develop an "enterprising solution" to the resourcing of your project. Maybe you can charge for your services. Maybe you can

"My biggest problem was shifting from well-paid freelance film work to an insecure existence doing what I wanted to do. It can sometimes be frustrating to know that other people are making millions as a result of exploiting people and the earth's natural resources, yet the ones wishing to fix the fallout often struggle to get by."

CYNDI RHOADES, ANTIAPATHY

get advertising or sponsorship. If Andrew Tew could raise $1million through a website to see him through college *(page 175)*, then there must be a "brilliant idea" you could develop which will bring in the money you need.

* In the UK, UnLtd – the Foundation for Social Entrepreneurs – makes "Level 1" awards to people to have a go at changing the world. Awards are offered averaging £2,500 and up to £5,000 to people over sixteen (there is a separate youth programme for people aged 11–25) who live in the UK where the project has some UK benefit. Many of the case studies in this book are UnLtd award winners. Level 2 awards of £20,000 are made to help people take their projects to the next stage.

www.unltd.org.uk

THREE PEOPLE RAISING MONEY

Do 26.2 of something

Make a marathon attempt to change the world. A marathon is 26.2 miles. And if you are prepared to run a marathon, a great way of raising money is to get people to sponsor you. *Just Giving* will provide you with your own web page for online giving.

But perhaps you are not able to run this distance or not fit enough to be happy doing it. The Multiple Sclerosis Resource Centre has been encouraging MS sufferers to raise money by doing 26.2 of something as a personal marathon challenge. Sylvie decided to walk on a treadmill for 26.2 minutes without a break.

"To be honest, I had no idea whether this was achievable, bearing in mind I only achieved 3 minutes on my first attempt! Each week I tried to extend the time I could manage. I soon realized that I had set the speed too fast at 0.7mph. It was the equivalent for me of climbing Mount Everest. So I had to slow it down just a little. I slowed the treadmill down to 0.5mph. On the third attempt, I achieved my dream of walking for the 26.2 minutes without a break. In the end I managed to raise a grand total of £2,227. Now, that's what I call remarkable!" – Sylvie

Ideas for marathon challenges

• Make 26 cups of tea, charging friends £1 a cup.

• Stand absolutely still for 26.2 minutes.

• Drink 26.2 pints of beer (spread over a few days!)

• Ask 26 friends or family to raise £10 each.

• Write letters to 26 friends you haven't been in touch with recently, asking them to contribute.

• Work in silence – everyone in the office is quiet for 26.2 minutes (except for answering the phone).

• Clean 26 cars, charging £5 a time.

• Collect 26 old mobile phones from friends and colleagues, and sell them via a recycling scheme.

• Do 26.2 minutes on the rowing machine or treadmill at your fitness club.

• Lose 26.2 lb and ask for £1-a-lb sponsorship

MULTIPLE SCLEROSIS RESOURCE CENTRE:
www.msrc.co.uk

JUST GIVING:
www.justgiving.com

THE LONG WAY HOME

Dover, UK to Cape Town, South Africa by motorbike

A girl, a bike, a dream . . . the journey of a lifetime . . . A website, a blog and a target of £5,000 for charity.

Sandi Langton had been planning a trans-Africa motorbike trip for more than four years. She decided to use her trip to raise £5,000 for Stand Up For Africa, which encourages young Africans to do something to better the lives of African children.

The money will go to support Safe Alternatives for Youth, to be used to educate the youth of the Kitamanyangamba slum in Kampala, where the school dropout rate is 80 per cent and there are high levels of crime, unwanted pregnancies and sexually transmitted diseases, including HIV/AIDS.

Sandi created a website and a blog which charts her progress, and organized online giving through **www.justgiving.com**

"Been doing my best to raise money, but not doing too marvelously YET. It isn't easy at all. Honestly, it's pretty hard. I've managed to sell some T-shirts and a few friends have made donations. Corporate sponsorship is complicated and takes time, and possibly more rejection than I feel up to. Mostly companies are prepared to give things not money. I guess we should find a way of turning their gifts into money so it can become bricks and mortar . . . which reminds me, I'd better ask BMW for an answer. It will probably be a NO, but I have to ask. I'm still sure we will raise the £5000 for the centre. I just want to be packed and off. Not long . . . "

http://long-way-home.com

www.standupforafrica.org.uk

THE OPERA WALK

Kathryn Harries is an opera singer. Thirty years ago she began raising money for charity by giving concerts and by walking. Concerts in 2005 and 2006 for East Sussex Hospices raised £74,000 and £75,000. Her John o' Groats to Land's End walk in 2001 for Speakability, the aphasia charity, raised £86,000. Christmas concerts she has put on for thirty years with the help of her operatic friends and ladies choir have raised over £400,000. She *"fully expects to be performing with the help of designer Zimmer frames in the not too distant future!"*

Kathryn came up with the idea for an Opera Walk while in France performing Janacek's opera *Katya Kabanova* for Lyon Opera. She was waiting for the lift chatting to John Graham Hall, chairman of the English National Opera Benevolent Fund, who had the role of Katya's poor, put-upon son. John asked Kathryn for her ideas for how to raise money for the fund. She heard herself say, "I could always go for another long walk". At that moment the Opera Walk was born, and Kathryn was committed to doing it.

The walk took place in late spring 2006. Kathryn walked 643 miles from London to Cardiff to Leeds and back to London in five weeks giving fourteen concerts in churches, concert halls, country houses, schools and community centres en route. Many of her friends in the opera world took part in the concerts, giving their services for free. It ended with a curtain call on the final night of *Ariodante* at the English National Opera. And a Grand Finale Gala Concert was held in November.

Over £50,000 was raised mainly through well-wishers sponsoring the walk and from the concerts along the route – the patrons list reads like a Who's Who of everyone in opera. Publicity and administrative support were given by the ENO and its staff. The walk was supported by Guy Salmon, Jaguar dealers, who provided a support vehicle and fuel vouchers.

NOTE: Aphasia robs its victim of the power of speech (to a greater or lesser degree). People with aphasia are often treated as if they are drunk and stupid. Because they have few or no words, they can't answer the phone, fill in forms, ask for help . . . People of all ages can become aphasic through head injury, brain surgery or a stroke.

www.kathrynharries.co.uk

THE OPERA WALK:

http://englishnationalopera.veriovps.co.uk/operawalk

CYCLING THE WORLD

International charity bike rides are extremely popular. Participants do an amazing challenge, such as cycle the length of the Great Wall of China or go around the Grand Canyon. They pay an entry fee, have a great time and raise lots of money. There is usually a minimum sponsorship requirement, with participants committing to raise perhaps £1,000 or £2,500.

It all started in 1991. War in the Middle East had hugely reduced tourism in Israel. Erich Reich had recently set up a tourism business specializing in Holy Land pilgrimages. He approached two charities – Ravenswood, a Jewish charity for people with severe learning disabilities, and the Edinburgh Medical Missionary Society (EMMI), a Christian charity running a Hospital in Nazareth – and suggested a Biblical Bike Ride from Dan to Beersheva in 1992.

Gordon Fox, a consultant to Ravenswood, agreed to take the idea forward. Ravenswood became lead charity and aimed to recruit 125 riders, EMMI promised seventy-five riders and the tourist company fifty more. Each rider would pay a refundable deposit of £75 and commit to raising £1,500 in sponsorship (which would more than cover the £500 per person cost). Ravenswood's target was £125,000; in

the event, Ravenswood had 165 riders raising an average of £3,000 each and £500,000 in total.

The ride was not only a huge fundraising success; everyone had a fantastic time. The benefits were more than just money. Ravenswood encouraged its beneficiaries to participate by riding tandem with a carer as the front seat rider. This gave them a huge personal fulfilment, and it gave all the other riders a better understanding of the value of Ravenswood's work. Many riders became loyal, committed Ravenswood supporters.

Many riders wanted to do another ride. In 1993, Gordon organized a second ride from Ashkelon (near Gaza) through the Negev to Eilat, this time for Ravenswood on its own. Over 300 cyclists took part, raising over £1 million.

Gordon expanded the Ravenswood challenge rides, organising four or more events a year in exciting locations around the world. Other charities jumped on the big event bandwagon, many such as the British Heart Foundation, the National Association for Deaf Children and Mencap placing advertisements in the national press to recruit riders and dreaming up ever more exotic routes for the rides.

EATING FOR A BETTER WORLD

Organizing big fundraising dinners is a risky business. A huge amount of money goes just to pay for the room and the food. Organizing dinners in people's homes is far less risky. You could even ask lots of people to host a dinner on the same night. Each host could cook and pay for the dinner as their contribution. Their guests enjoy themselves and make a donation. Here are some examples:

One day: Hugh Evans, started the Oaktree Foundation to raise money for educational projects in South Africa. His "Dinners for Life" event in 2005 raised over $130,000 from dinners hosted by well-wishers all over the world. Oaktree has now changed the format to "One Day", when its supporters are encouraged to organize different types of events all on the same day.
www.theoaktree.org

1000 dinners: Adopt-a-Minefield has a 1000 Dinners Campaign, where dinners are hosted each year between 1 March, in commemoration of the signing of the Mine Ban Treaty, and 4 April, in support of International Mine Awareness Day. Part of the money raised comes from games played by the guests (instructions are on the website).
http://landmines.org.uk/1000+dinners

Chain dinners: The Global Fund for Women encourages supporters to organize a "chain dinner". Twelve people are invited to dinner and pay $12. Two people from amongst the guests agree to invite twelve people to another dinner . . . each of these will then get two people from their two dinners to invite twelve more people . . . and so on. The original dinner raises $12 x 12 = $144. The next two dinners raise 2 x $12 x 12 = $288. The next four dinners raise 4 x $12 x 12 = $576 . . . Of course, not all the people who agree to host a dinner will actually do so; and like all chains it will eventually peter out. But it's a great idea.
www.globalfundforwomen.org

Hunger banquets: If you are fighting hunger, it is inappropriate for people to feast themselves. So Oxfam America has developed the idea of a Hunger Banquet which mirrors wealth and poverty in the world. Each person attending is randomly assigned a role, which determines what they eat.

• 15 per cent are in **high income;** they sit at a table and enjoy a three-course meal with wine and all the trimmings.

• 25 per cent are in **middle income**; they sit on chairs and eat rice and beans (delicious and nutritious).

• 60 per cent are the **world's poor;** they sit on the floor, and get only rice and water. They will suffer the fate of the billions of poor people throughout the world who go to bed hungry each night.

Organize a hunger banquet to raise money. Invite nineteen people. Ask each to contribute £10 or $20. But then ask the rich pay more!

www.hungerbanquet.org

www.oxfamamerica.org

ACTION GUIDE: FUNDRAISING

1. DRAWING UP A BUDGET

You have already produced an action plan for getting your project started *(see page 110)* – this sets out all the activities you will be undertaking. Now you need to work out a budget – which puts a cost on everything in your plan.

Doing this will be extremely helpful:

- Your budget helps you specify *exactly what you need*.

- The budgeting process enables you to question all the costs ... and so ensure they are necessary. This will *make your project more cost effective*.

- You know exactly how much you need to raise, and what you will be spending the money on. This *makes the fundraising very much easier*.

- Your budget enables you to *monitor your progress* ... and take action if things are not going to plan.

This is the budgeting process:

Step 1: Work out a plan of action

Describe the activities you will undertake either to complete your project (if you are producing a budget for your project) or over the next year (if you are producing an annual budget). Make sure you include everything you plan to do.

Step 2: Make a list of each item you need for your project

Itemize the things you need to purchase; services and facilities you need; anything else you can think of. You can put an overall sum for some items, such as publicity, and then decide later how you will spend the money.

Step 3: Make an estimate of each item on your list

Get estimates from suppliers. For bigger items get more than one estimate. For the smaller items, an informed guess will often do.

Step 4: Calculate the cost of staff time

If staff are being employed, work out the salary cost per day and the number of days for each person involved. Then double the cost per day to allow for all the meetings, non-productive work and holidays. If you don't do this, you will always be asking for too little.

Step 5: Add something for contingencies

Things never work out quite as planned, so it is sensible to add an amount to pay for things you have forgotten or where they cost more than you budgeted; 10 per cent will usually be enough for contingencies.

Step 6: Add something for general overheads

What you have done so far is estimate your **direct costs**. You also need to include your **indirect costs**. There is the cost of your office and all the stationery, postage and other supplies you are purchasing, and there is the cost of running your organization (everything from holding management meetings to producing annual accounts). Include a contribution to your office and organization costs. Just make a reasonable estimate based on the size of the project in relation to all the work that your organization is doing and its running costs. This might add an extra 25 per cent to your costs.

Step 7: Add all this up to produce a total

Discuss your draft budget with everyone involved in the project. Make any adjustments.

Can you justify each item in your budget? Then ask yourself whether the cost is reasonable in relationship to the work being done. If not, find ways of economising. Agree this as your final budget.

Step 8: Think about which items you could get donated

This will reduce the amount of money you need to raise. Draw up a "Wish List" of what you want donated. Then just ask.

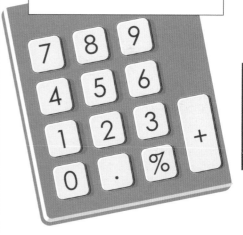

Problems to avoid

Missing items: It is extremely easy to forget items of expenditure and leave them out of the budget. Try to do your best to include everything.

Seriously underestimating your costs: This is a frequent problem – partly because people are too optimistic, and partly because they are frightened of constructing a budget which seems too high. Make sure that you put some real effort into estimating all the larger items as accurately as you can.

Allowing for inflation: Some budgets are for more than one year. In which case, the costs in year 2 onwards will be affected by inflation. This will not be too much of a problem during periods of low inflation; but it can be serious if inflation starts to rise.

Risk and contingencies: Think about what can go wrong. And then what you could do to minimize the risk. If you are organizing an event which is dependent on the weather, for example, you might want to consider paying for insurance

---

Budget worksheet

Items needed	Estimated cost	Tick if it will be donated
1.	.... □	
2.	.... □	
3.	.... □	
4.	.... □	
5.	.... □	
6.	.... □	
7.	.... □	
8.	.... □	

Estimated project costs: ....

Cost of staff
Number of staff: ....
Number of days: ....
Daily rate to be charged: ....

Staff + project costs: ....
Contingencies: Add 10%   ....
Office costs: ....
Management and supervision   ....

TOTAL: ....

2.
SOME WAYS OF RAISING MONEY QUICKLY

Fundraising takes time. You need to identify people to approach and do some basic research on what they might be interested in supporting before you send them a proposal. Then you may have to wait weeks or months to get a decision on whether they are prepared to support you. But you may need money now. Here are ten ideas for raising small amounts quite quickly.

1. Give it yourself: This is the easiest way of raising money. If it's for something you really believe in, it can be extremely satisfying to spend your money this way.

2. Earn the money: Take a part-time job, run errands in return for donations, or designate a part of your income (such as speaker fees or book royalties) for your cause.

3. Raise money from friends, family and colleagues at work: They will support you because they know you and because you ask them to.

4. If you yourself **give a part of the** total (say 10 per cent), you can **ask your friends to match it.** Find nine people prepared to do this, and you'll have all you need.

5. Collect together things you no longer need, and **sell them at a car boot sale or on eBay.** Ask your friends to do the same. Turn a mountain of unwanted items into cash for your cause.

6. Organize a reception or a drinks evening, and ask lots of people to come. Ask them to contribute a fixed amount for coming. Provide pledge forms, and ask them to give a bit more.

7. Ask several friends to **organize fundraising dinners for their friends** *(see page 151).*

8. Ask a celebrity to do something for you – attend a fundraising event as guest of honour, offer their house or garden for an event, donate an item to sell in an auction... Ask celebrities you know. Pluck up your courage, ask a celebrity who lives locally, even if you've never met them,

9. Collect gifts in kind: Go down the high street asking local shops and businesses to contribute something for your auction. Many will be happy to give you something. Your job is then to turn these gifts into cash.

10. Apply to a small grants fund: These will have simple applications procedures and quick turnaround times. If you live in the UK, check out UnLtd **(www.unltd.org. uk),** Awards for All **(www.awardsforall. org.uk),** YouthBank (for youth projects, **www.yyouthbank.org.uk)** and your local council (which may have a Community Chest small grants scheme).

Fundraising

3.
GETTING THINGS DONATED

Getting things donated is often easier than raising the cash.

People may have something that they no longer need or which they can make available to you very easily. It may even cost them a lot less than a cash donation. Asking companies and individuals to give in kind makes a lot of sense.

Here are some of the things that you can try to get donated:

• **Used equipment,** such as a computer or a fax machine or office furniture. Someone else's cast off could be just what you are looking for!

• **Facilities,** such as a room to hold an event – a boardroom for an important meeting, training facilities to run a workshop, or a reception area to hold a party.

• **Professional services,** such as help with advertising and PR, accountancy, management consultancy (for drawing up a business plan), legal advice, a surveyor, etc. Someone or some company may be able to provide you with what you need.

• **The use of equipment,** such as photocopying equipment to produce a report, or video-conferencing facilities to hold a consultation.

• **A company's products,** either provided as a gift or loaned to you, either for you to use or to turn into cash through an auction or some other fundraising event.

• **Raw materials** that a company uses or offcuts which would otherwise be thrown away.

Making a Wish List

Here is a good way of getting gifts in kind:

1. First, **make a list of everything you need** – this is called your "Wish List". You could divide this into "*Must Haves*" and "*Would Likes*". Concentrate on getting what you must have. But you may find that you are also able to get some of the other things on your list.

2. Then **write down the names of companies and individuals** who have what you need. These are the people you will ask. Find out the name and contact details of the person who is able to make a decision – whoever he or she is. If you are already known to that person or if you can get an introduction, that will make things much easier.

3. Next **ask.** Writing letters (or sending emails) does not work well. Most unsolicited letters will not be read. The best way of asking is by telephone, or in the case of local shops by calling round. Tell them that you hope to get a lot of good publicity, and that you will make sure that people will hear about their generosity. Tell them that you could have asked for a cash donation, but this is a much cheaper and easier option for them.

4. Have a fallback position. If someone is unable to give you what you are asking for, then suggest something else. This will improve your chances of getting something in return for the effort you are putting in. Here are some ideas:

"*. . . last year's model or something that a customer has returned would be perfectly OK for us.*"

"*. . . if you can't donate it, please give us a big discount? Why don't we go halves?*"

"*. . . I'm really sorry you can't help us this time. But do you know anyone who could?*" Then you can telephone their contact saying you are ringing at so-and-so's suggestion.

5. Once you've got something donated, **say thank you.** Tell them how important the donation was to you and what good use you made of it. They might like to support you again.

My wish list

What I would like

Who I'm going to ask

Their contact details

How I'm going to approach them

4. WHO HAS THE MONEY?

Next you have to think about where you are going to get the money from. It will probably come from one of these sources:

1. Individuals

family, friends, colleagues at work

people who have supported you before

rich individuals (if you can find them)

people known to have some sort of interest in what you are doing

2. The general public

street and house-to-house collections

people contacting you because of media coverage

direct mail (sending out lots of letters to mailing lists, or inserting a flyer in a magazine or newspaper)

people you meet (remember to have a leaflet to give them)

the person behind you in the supermarket check out

3. Fundraising events

entertainment events

participation events

market stalls and garage sales

auctions, raffles, sweepstakes and lotteries

4. Small grants

small grants schemes and
community chests

local trusts and foundations

local companies

5. Larger grants

trusts and foundations

local government

government grants programmes

business sponsorship

6. Earned income

charging for your services or the use
of your facilities

sale of publications, T-shirts,
greetings cards and other
merchandise

some sort of business activity that
will generate a profit

How I plan to raise the money

Step 1: Think about how you will get the money and who might be interested
in supporting you.

Step 2: Draw up an income budget, setting out how much you plan to get
from different sources. Try to do a few things really well, rather do too many
different things. Build on your contacts, your expertise and any opportunities
you discover.

Now use this to create a plan of action for your fundraising.

Source	How much
1.	
2.	
3.	
4.	
5.	
Total	

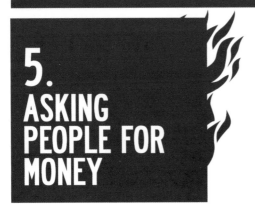

5. ASKING PEOPLE FOR MONEY

There are two rules for fundraising success:

Rule 1: In order to raise the money you need, you have to ask. This may seem obvious. But there are a lot of people who think a lot about ways of raising the money they need, but then never get around to asking anybody!

Rule 2: When you ask, make sure you ask effectively. People may already believe that the issue is important. Or you might have to persuade them. Be enthusiastic about what you are doing, and share your dreams with them. They will be supporting *you* as much as your project. The important thing is to create a sense of excitement, *so that they will want to give.*

Tell people WHAT

What the problem is

What you plan to do about it

What you hope to achieve

But also tell people WHY

Why it is really important to do something about the problem

Why something needs to be done *now*

Why your ideas provide a really good way of addressing the need

Why *you* are the right person to back

And also tell them what's in it for them. Whoever you are approaching, think about it from their point of view. Why will they want to support you? Will they want anything back in return for handing over their money?

Some tips

• **Appeal to people's emotions.** Show examples of real people and how you are changing their lives.

• **Link the donation to something specific** you will do (such as paying for an eye operation to restore sight to one child).

• **Listen** and try to answer any questions.

• **Encourage people to give generously.** Suggest an annual or even a monthly donation paid by Standing Order. Give examples of what other people have given.

• **Show how small amounts can make a big difference.** People can get a lot more satisfaction by helping make a better world than going out for another indifferent meal!

• **Don't give up.** Be persistent. Remain optimistic. If somebody turns you down, go and find someone else to ask.

Do it now!

It's actually quite easy to make a good case. Think about what you will say, and then find people to ask.

• **Ask somebody today.** It's never too soon to get started. Contact someone and arrange to meet later on today. Then tell them about your plans and invite them to support you.

• **Ask somebody tomorrow.** Get into the habit of asking.

Some good reasons for supporting you

"We're going to sort the problem out for good."

"We will be helping lots and lots of people."

"What we are doing really works." Or "It's a completely new idea, that nobody's thought of before."

"Lots of other people are already supporting us."

"It's local. We're dealing with a problem on your doorstep."

"Your support will make all the difference."

"We're really cost-effective. We'll give you the biggest bang for your buck!"

6. WRITING A FUNDRAISING APPLICATION

If you want to apply for a grant from a foundation or a government source or a company's charitable budget, you usually have to send in a written proposal or complete an application form.

Before you put pen to paper, you need to do these three things:

Step 1: Decide who to approach

Draw up a "hit list" of possibilities. Get information from published funding directories and from the Internet. Ask other people for their suggestions.

Step 2: Do some research

Once you have decided who might be interested, find out about their grants policies (what they like to support, and what they say they will *not* support). Find out about the application procedure – how much information is required, how it should be submitted, whether there are any deadlines for receipt of applications.

Step 3: Decide what and how much to apply for

Think about whether there is a particular aspect of your project that they might particularly like to support. If so, request support for that. Think also about how much they are likely to give. Look at some of the previous grants they have made; this will give you an indication of both their interest and the scale of their giving.

What to include in your application

Often there are guidelines specifying what information is required; if this is the case, then give them the information they need. If there is an application form, make sure you answer *all* the questions properly.

It's best to create a structure for your application, going from problem to solution. Use this as a template:

• **A project title**. Make it catchy.

• **Introduce yourself.** Tell them what you do and why you are writing to them. Show them that you are a really great organization.

• **State the problem or need.** Give them the basic facts.

• **Say what you propose to do.** Describe your project and its main objectives.

• **Say how you will do it**. Describe your plan of action.

- **Tell them what you hope to achieve.** Specify some targets, then try your best to achieve these.

- **Say how much you need**. Provide an overall figure. You can attach a detailed budget to your application.

- **Say where you intend to get the rest of the money from.** You may need to get more than one grant, and some of the money might come from income you earn.

- **Ask.** If possible, ask for a specific amount.

- **Give them some reasons why they might be interested.**

- **Think a little about how the project might be funded in the longer term.** Share your thoughts on this. Most want to see that your project has a chance of continuing.

- **Sign off.** Say you are happy to send them more information or answer their questions. Invite them to visit you to see your work and to meet some of your beneficiaries.

Six tips for a successful application

1. Try to get yourself known about before you apply. If people have already heard about your work, or if they have visited you and been impressed, this will improve your chances.

2. Personalize the application as much as you can. This is not just a matter of "topping" it with a donor's name and address, but more about making sure that it reflects their interests, and suggests why they might like to fund it. Applications which look like circulars almost certainly end up in the bin.

3. Make sure it is **written in plain language** and **not too long**. Don't use jargon or long words or long paragraphs. Use a red pencil to strike out irrelevant waffle.

4. Make sure it is **neat and tidy.** It doesn't have to be glossy, but it should look professional.

5. Make sure it is **error-free.** Proofread it for typos. See that the budget adds up. Some funders are just looking for an excuse for *not* funding you. Don't give them this opportunity!

6. Make sure you give the **name and contact details** of someone who can be contacted to discuss the application . . . and if that person isn't you, that they are properly briefed.

7.
ORGANIZING A COLLECTION

Collecting small sums from lots of people can produce a lot of money.

Collecting in the street is a traditional way of doing this – and you will usually need some sort of permit from your local council, who will also be able to tell you the rules for how to run your collection.

Going house-to-house, knocking on doors, asking if people are interested in hearing about your work . . . and in contributing something or becoming a member . . . this is a really good idea for local projects. It also gets you known in the local community.

Collecting on buses and trains. There is a captive audience, and for a good cause they may be generous. Strictly speaking, you'll need permission, but . . .

But there are lots of other ways of collecting money from your family, friends, colleagues at work and the general public.

You may require some materials and equipment (such as collecting boxes). You should be able to find specialist suppliers in Yellow Pages or on Google. Or you can make your own.

If you are knocking on doors or organizing a flag day, you will require lots of volunteers. They need to be shown how to collect – stand in a prominent place, smile, make eye contact, invite people to come and hear about your organization. They will also need to be properly briefed, in case they are asked questions (which they will be). Draw up a list of FAQs which give them the answers.

If people seem really interested, make sure you get their name and contact details. You can send them further information, copies of your newsletter or e-newsletter, and invite them along to events.

Ten more ways of collecting money:

Idea 1: Save your small change. Each night put the coins in your pocket (or at least the smaller ones) into a jar. You will save quite a lot without even noticing it. Ask your friends to do the same.

Idea 2: Organize a "Dress Down Friday" at your workplace or in your school or college. Each Friday people can turn up in causal clothes provided they contribute a small sum. *"Go Green Day"* is a variation on this. People turn up in green clothes to show their support for the environment, and are asked to contribute £1 – you could ask those that don't to pay a £2 "fine" (but you will have to persuade them).

Idea 3: Hold a Rag Day. Dress up in fancy dress, be really cheerful and go out on the streets with a lot of friends to collect money. Use buckets for people to toss in their loose change. Smile a lot and ask people to be generous.

Idea 4: Collect at your local supermarket or shopping centre. Lots of people go shopping at weekends, so these are great places to have a collection. You need to ask the manager beforehand. A similar idea is to collect at sporting events, such as football matches – inside the stadium at half time, outside before and after the match.

Idea 5: Have a swear box at work, and devise a range of fines for all the different swear words.

Idea 6: Ask a restaurant to add an optional £1 to each bill for a month as a special promotion. Most customers won't object, and this can get the restaurant quite a lot of good publicity.

Idea 7: Go on a pub crawl. Go from pub to pub, bar to bar. Ask the manager if you can collect from the customers. If it's a good cause and a season of goodwill, they may well agree.

Idea 8: Organize a "Flag Day", where collectors stand in a busy shopping street with a tray of stickers or ribbons that people make a contribution for. Those who are wearing them are those who have supported you.

Idea 9: Put a large collecting box in your toilet, and a note on the door for guests suggesting that they put some money in the box.

Idea 10: Ask shopkeepers to place a collecting box near the cashpoint. Most purchases do not add up to nice round sums, so this is a good way for people to get rid of their unwanted small change.

8.

ORGANIZING AN ENTERTAINMENT EVENT

Organizing an event can be a really good way of raising money.

People will come along because they already support you... or because they are interested in what you are doing... or just because they want to participate in the event.

Create the right event, get lots of people to come, ensure that there is a good atmosphere, run the event well . . . then you should be able to generate a lot of money.

How to organize a successful event

1. Decide the **type of event** you want to organize (dinner, dance, quiz evening, auction . . .).

2. Have **clear objectives.** Why are you doing it? To raise money? Entertain supporters? Get publicity?

3. Think up a **catchy title.**

4. Decide **who to invite . . .** and how many you want to come.

5. Decide **the programme.** Who would you like as speakers and celebrities? How will you get to them?

6. Decide **the venue.** Is it suitable and available? How many people does it hold? Is it wheelchair accessible?

7. Decide **the date.** Do this sooner rather than later.

8. Check whether you need any **official permissions or insurance cover.**

9. Think about the **equipment** you will need . . . and where you will get it from. Will you need **banners and decorations?**

10. Will you be **providing refreshments.** Who will do this? Will you charge?

11. **How will you publicize the event?** What **posters** and **publicity material** will you need?

12. How many **helpers** will you need on the day. What will you ask them to do? Who will be responsible for briefing, coordinating and thanking them?

13. Who will be the **organizing team?** What will each person's responsibilities be? One person should have overall responsibility for the event and ensuring its success.

14. Agree a **budget.** Keep costs to an absolute minimum. Beg or borrow as much as you can.

Four more bits of advice

1. **Estimate how many people will come.** Then do your best to get even more.

2. **Avoid risk.** It's easier to spend money than to raise it. Do what you can to cut costs and think of additional ways to generate income (such as an auction at a fundraising dinner).

3. **Keep a record of everyone who came.** They might be interested in supporting you or coming to another event.

4. **Hold a de-briefing session immediately afterwards.** Learn from experience. Do it better next time.

An A-to-Z of fundraising ideas

Auction of dreams
Barbecues
Christmas parties
Concerts and cabarets
Discos and balls
Elvis look-alike competitions
Fashion shows
Green gatherings
Halloween parties
Indoor markets
Jumble sales
Karaoke evenings
Lantern parades
Masked balls
Non-violent movie marathons
Open days
Picnics in the park
Quiz evenings
Raffles and tombolas
Scrabble parties
Tours and visits
Ugly face competitions
Village fetes
Whist drives and bridge evenings
Youth festivals
Zero-emissions challenges

Tori, a twenty-one-year-old who is hooked on travel, has compiled an A–Z of fundraising ideas. Add your own ideas to her list:
www.gapyear.com/fundraising/a_z_of_fundraising_ideas.html

Sarah Hartwell and friends have compiled another A to Z:
http://messybeast.com/moggycat/fundraise.htm

9.
ORGANIZING A SPONSORED EVENT

There are all sorts of ideas for a sponsored event: a marathon, a long walk, a jog (or fun run), a swim, pick up litter, lose weight, stop smoking.

Participants ask friends, family and colleagues to make a contribution for each mile or circuit they complete, each sack of litter they collect, each kilo they lose, each day they continue not to smoke. Some of the people asked will prefer to make a lump sum contribution. You organize the event; and they do the hard work of asking; you get the money.

Get all your friends and supporters to participate. Some will do so because they want to support what you are doing, others because they are attracted to the activity. Lots of people will be asking lots of other people to give small amounts. This soon adds up to a lot of money.

To make a sponsored event work, you need to:

* **Decide on an event.** Something that helps promote your cause is always a good idea.

* **Find lots of people** who are willing to participate.

* **Agree a target with them** for the number of sponsors they will get and the amount they will try to raise.

* Provide them with **sponsorship forms and publicity material.**

* Keep in touch and **give them encouragement.**

* **Hold the event** – make sure it's organized really well.

* After the event, **make sure that they collect all the money** they were promised and that they hand it over to you.

Check out the Just Giving service for charity fundraising. They provide web pages for people to raise money with credit card donations with the tax relief being processed online. **www.justgiving.com**

Planning your event

How will you get your participants? Who will you ask and how will you get hold of them?

Who will be the organizing team? And what will be their particular responsibilities?

Where is the venue and what permissions do you need (this is important if you are using a public space)?

How many helpers will you need on the day, and who will you ask?

What publicity material will you need (posters, T-shirts, leaflets, sponsorship forms, etc.)?

What is the "unit" of sponsorship (circuits, miles, etc.), and how many units is each participant expected to complete?

10. MORE FUNDRAISING IDEAS

Auctions

Auctions are a good way of raising money. You need:

- Lots of **interesting and desirable things to sell;** many you can get donated.

- A **lively outgoing person** to act as auctioneer.

- **Lots of people** who come along and bid generously.

You can auction lots of things:

- **Things that you get donated** – such as free holidays from a travel company or flights from an airline (ring up); a case of wine from a wine merchant; a meal for two at a local restaurant; or a hamper of nice things to eat from a deli (just call round and ask)... The trick is to find things people really want that actually cost the supplier very little.

- **Things that you persuade people to do for you** that money can't buy. A dinner for two with a famous pop star you know; a week at someone's fabulous holiday home in the West Indies; a day shadowing a government minister... This is sometimes called an "auction of dreams".

- **Things that people agree to do.** Mow your lawn once a week, babysit five times; serenade you and your loved one as part of a romantic evening. All these will have a value to somebody.

Here are two other ways of turning in-kind donations into cash:

- A raffle or prize draw. People buy a ticket, and the winning tickets are drawn.

- A tombola. Each ticket purchased wins a prize.

Selling things

It's usually easier to ask for money than to earn it by selling things. But here are some things you can sell (some you can make as well) to raise money:

Seasonal items

☐ Christmas cards

☐ Calendars

Promotional items

☐ Tee shirts

☐ Posters

☐ Badges

Handicrafts

☐ Jewellery

☐ Scented candles

☐ Small artworks

Food and drink

☐ Biscuits and cakes

☐ Sweets and jams

11.
SAYING THANK YOU

It's really important to thank people for the support they have given you . . . and then keep in touch. They have supported you. They will be interested in seeing how things are going. If you begin to develop a good relationship with them, then they might want to give again – perhaps even more next time!

Remember to thank your supporters. It is surprising how many people fail to do this. Do it as soon as you receive the donation. Write a letter to them personally.

Some ways of saying thank you . . .

- **Ring up** and tell them how thrilled you are with their support

- **Send a text message** or **an email**

- **Write a formal thank you letter** . . . perhaps with a hand-written note at the bottom saying how much you appreciate their generosity. Remember to post the letter!

Six tips for getting your supporters more involved

1. Tell them when you have raised all the money you need.

2. Report back regularly telling them what you have done and how well you have used their money.

3. Keep proper accounts. Tell your supporters what you have raised and how you have spent it. This is called "being transparent".

4. Invite them to come and see what you are doing and to meet the people you are working with.

5. Organize a thank you party after the project has ended to celebrate your achievements. You could invite a celebrity to welcome everybody.

6. Take photographs and write up case studies that illustrate the impact you have been able to make.

Fundraising

171

Chapter 6

World domination

Your project could become really successful. It could be replicated all over your country, perhaps even all over the world. You might even win a Right Livelihood Award or the Nobel Peace Prize. A great idea that meets a real need... oh, and a lot of hard work... that is all it takes!

GO OUT AND CONQUER THE WORLD

Twenty-four-year-old Sarah Greaves set up art reaching communities to run art projects for children in deprived countries and to exchange artwork internationally to increase inter-cultural awareness.

Sarah's idea was basically very simple. In many countries, schools are so short of resources that they can do little more than just deliver the curriculum (if that). Yet in the rich world, we know that experiential learning and encouraging children's creativity are important. Sarah wanted to organize a creative arts "summer school" for Kenyan children.

In August 2004, Sarah took two artists to work with children in a Kenyan orphanage. She asked them to do this for free and to pay their way; and they were happy to do this. For doing this, Sarah received a Young Achiever Award. At the awards ceremony, Sarah was interviewed by June Sarpong, a well-known TV presenter, who asked her what her future plans were. Sarah replied with two words: "World domination".

If you've had a great idea, tried it out and found a way of making it work, the next step is to spread the idea. You can scale it up and build a successful organization nationally or even internationally. Or perhaps you just want to inspire others to go out and do what you have done.

Either way you will be multiplying your impact on the problem. You may then be ready to start on your next idea!

How to become a guru

Inspire other people, and you can create a movement for change.

Whether it is a campaign for real ale or a "small is beautiful" approach to technology, promote your ideas widely and encourage others to take them up. Political leaders know this. Religious leaders know this too. Why shouldn't leaders of social change adopt a similar strategy?

To become a leader, you need to get yourself some followers. The following will help:

- A great idea which is "right for the time".

- A charismatic personality with "the gift of the gab".

- Dressing all in white (you will appear god-like!).

- A few existing acolytes, as this will encourage others to join.

Don't pay your supporters (which some political parties do), as this is an unsustainable strategy.

If you find the key to becoming a successful guru, write a how-to book about it. There's a gap in the market!

An Idea Worth a Million Dollars

Alex was twenty-one. He needed to pay for his college studies, and didn't like the idea of student debt. It took Alex just ten minutes to come up with a good idea for doing this.

He would create the Million Dollar Home Page selling pixels to advertisers in squares of 10 x 10. There would be 10,000 squares, each providing just enough space to display a logo or a short message. Clicking on the square would take the visitor to the advertiser's website. Advertisers could buy as many squares as they liked. Alex promised to maintain the website for at least five years.

Alex sold all one million pixels within four months, and raised his $1 million. He then started on his next project – to sell another one million pixels, this time at $2 each. Half the $2 million will be given as one prize of $1 million to be awarded randomly to a visitor to the site who has clicked on one of the advertisements (which advertisement will also be selected at random). This will encourage people to click on as many advertisements as they can to give themselves a better chance of winning the prize. Alex will keep $900,000 as his cut (which will also cover his costs), and $100,000 will be donated to a charity of the prizewinner's choice. Alex's growing reputation and lots of good publicity should ensure its success.

But what's this got to do with changing the world? Directly, not a lot. But indirectly, you could (a) adapt Alex's brilliant idea to help you raise money to change the world (why not a Green Homepage with pixel ads focusing on sustainable living?) and (b) you might now feel that with a great idea plus a great fundraising idea, you will be unbeatable.

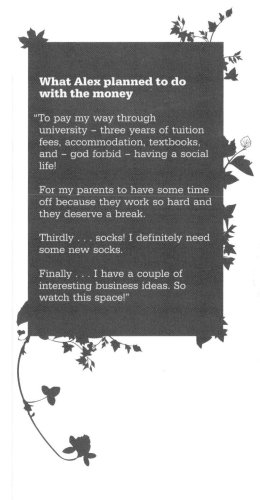

What Alex planned to do with the money

"To pay my way through university – three years of tuition fees, accommodation, textbooks, and – god forbid – having a social life!

For my parents to have some time off because they work so hard and they deserve a break.

Thirdly . . . socks! I definitely need some new socks.

Finally . . . I have a couple of interesting business ideas. So watch this space!"

ALEX'S PIXEL PAGES:

www.milliondollarhomepage.com and www.pixelotto.com

PROMOTING WELL-BEING

According to the World Health Organisation, by 2020 depression will be the leading cause of disability and the second biggest contributor to illness in the developed world, after coronary heart disease.

Promoting well-being is becoming a health priority. Here are stories of three young people who decided to do something to promote well-being, each developing their own solutions based on their own experience and ideas. Each has the potential to "change the world".

Helping people through depression

Mark Swift: I am twenty-five years old. I grew up in St Helens, a former industrial town in north-west England. I was the first in my family to go to university, getting a degree in biochemistry from Liverpool University. Despite my academic success, I had been struggling for some time with low self-esteem.

After I enrolled on a doctoral programme, my depression began to spiral out of control. I spent the next two years trying to regain my self-confidence. I volunteered for a local mental health charity, which gave me a sense of purpose. As my confidence grew, new opportunities presented themselves. I eventually landed a job as a Mental Health Promotion Officer.

Because of my own experience, I had become passionate about helping people

who were experiencing mental health distress to recover and move forward with their lives. So in my free time, I started the Wellbeing Project. This is based on the idea that mental fitness is promoted by a combination of a balanced diet, exercise and relaxation, purposeful employment, spiritual development, support networks and relationships, recreational activity and sleep.

We provide a range of products, services and materials to help people rebuild their lives. We recruit people who have experienced mental health distress, so that their insights and experiences can be used to benefit others. The volunteering and employment through our programme itself creates a pathway to recovery, and helps people rebuild their lives.

www.wellbeingproject.co.uk

Changing the way people think about mental health

Jason Pegler: I was a high achiever at school. In 1993 at the age of seventeen, I was diagnosed with manic depression. I wrote a memoir of what I went through, to help other seventeen-year-olds who were experiencing similar problems. I produced and published this in 2002 under the title *A Can of Madness.*

"Do you want to know what it's like to be crazy, mad, loopy? Well I'm about to tell you. I'm also going to tell you how it feels to be suicidal for months on end – the fate of the manic. One thing, however, is for sure: the sooner you kill mania, the better. For you're a danger to yourself and other people when you don't know what you're doing."

I then went on to set up Chipmunka Publishing which is "the world's first Mental Health Publisher" in order to change the way people think about mental health. Chipmunka has published over 100 paperbacks and 400 e-books – 95 per cent of the titles are written by people experiencing mental health issues.

Jason has become a leading mental health activist, writer, rapper, public speaker and consultant on anything that promotes a positive image on mental health. In 2005 he won the New Statesman's Young Social Entrepreneur of the Year Award.

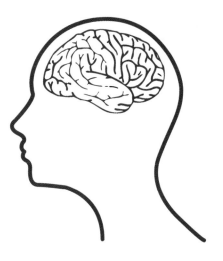

http://chipmunkapublishing.co.uk

Making complementary therapies available

Boo Armstrong: I was born in 1974 in west London. I became active pretty early on. My mum let a local homeless man come and use our bath, my granddad was a fundraiser for Barnados, and my family was full of teachers and other public servants. These were my role models for being actively engaged in my community.

By the beginning of secondary school I was a committed vegetarian, pretty focused on animal rights, and the local coordinator for an environmental group which collected paper for recycling, which generated money to plant trees.

Twenty years later I am trying to make complementary medicine available to everyone through the National Health Service, so that it is not just available to those who can afford to pay for it privately. The NHS budget is now more than £100 billion a year and is not providing medicine which is cheap and often effective – acupuncture,

osteopathy and other complementary treatments. I gave up my job running a local community health centre and started Get Well UK in 2002 to change all that.

The next big issue that I want to address is trauma. Many people in the UK have been traumatized to a greater or lesser extent – sexual and physical abuse of children, neglect, domestic violence, bullying, rape, persecution and extreme poverty. People are living with huge levels of unresolved issues and too many are using drugs and alcohol as an escape, rather than addressing the issues, and cycles of violence are repeating through the generations. I want to live in and help create a society based on peace in our homes and communities.

www.getwelluk.com

DARE TO START A SCHOOL

All over the developed world, we are told about the importance of education and how we must develop a "brain economy" if we are to thrive. The UK press writes about the billions poured into education, the continuing efforts to raise school standards and the joys of teaching as a profession.

To become a head teacher requires time, ambition and ability. If you have a couple of million to spare, you might even think about sponsoring your very own school – perhaps a City Academy named after you.

In the developing world, just providing affordable education to every child is a priority. And it is possible with very little money to make something happen. Here are the stories of three people who want to see that every child gets an education.

Making Universal Secondary Education feasible

The Millennium Development Goals agreed in 2000 to aim to achieve universal primary education by 2015. But what will happen to children educated up to Standard 6? Where will they go? What will they do? They are still children, and too young to start work.

This is the issue that two young men in their twenties, John Rendel and Mike Kironde, wanted to address. They wanted to open a secondary school in the slums of Kampala, in Uganda.

John spent two months in Uganda in 2002 before graduating from Oxford University in 2003. He met Mike who was determined to do better than his father, whose life was cut short by AIDS. Together they set up PEAS (Promoting Equality in African Schools).

They started their first school on a plot of land in Kampala offered to them by the Church of Uganda. By using existing buildings and building some new ones, the cost of starting this school was just £7,000. The school opened with twenty-four staff, and 120 students enrolled. It has grown. It now educates 900 students with fifty-two staff.

The aim is to run the school from the very modest fees charged (about a quarter of the fee levels of government schools). There are also some income-generating projects to create a bit more revenue. The first of these is a "Matatu" or shared taxi which is run commercially when not used for ferrying students.

Mike oversees the building works, ensures that the schools run well and manages their budgets. John returned to England, and after graduating, enrolled in Teach First – a scheme that encourages graduates to teach first before embarking on their chosen career.

As a Teach First teacher, John developed Bridges to Africa, which involves students from London schools doing a sponsored walk over London's bridges – 900 London students, many of them of African origin, participated in 2006 and raised £20,000 for PEAS. The fundraising will be extended to Birmingham and Manchester. All the participants are given support materials to find out about educational issues in Africa (as part of their citizenship studies). Some are now so enthusiastic that they are planning visit the school or spend a gap year volunteering in Uganda.

Back in Uganda, John and Mike have now opened five schools and are educating 3,000 Ugandans! They are now thinking about the next problem: where are the jobs for the young people who finish their education? So they are introducing enterprise education and experimenting with the idea of a business plan competition where students will win awards for their ideas for an enterprise.

If two twenty-somethings can provide education for 3,000 Ugandans, it shouldn't be impossible to offer secondary education to all Ugandans, and to all young people in Africa. Perhaps John and Mike have invented the idea of "Universal Secondary Education", something that even UNICEF and Oxfam haven't yet managed to start working on.

How an illiterate orange-seller saved money and built a school

Harekala Nyupadpu Hajabba is forty-five. He lives and works in Mangalore, a port city on the south-west coast of India. Hajabba is an orange-seller at the bus station, tempting thirsty travellers with fresh fruit. He is also illiterate. But at the end of 2004 he was named "Man of the Year" for Karnataka State.

Over the years, Hajabba had saved Rupee after Rupee for his dream project – to build a school for poor children in his village, which is 20 km from Mangalore. He wanted to ensure that no child from his village would grow up illiterate as he had done.

Hajabba's school opened in 2004, with fifty-six girl and sixty-five boy students. There is no big memorial board celebrating Hajabba's generosity. He is an anonymous donor. Hajabba is now saving to provide a playground for the school and to get electricity connected.

As "Man of the Year", Hajabba received $2,000. He could inspire others to make good Universal Primary Education a reality.

SOCIAL ENTREPRENEURSHIP

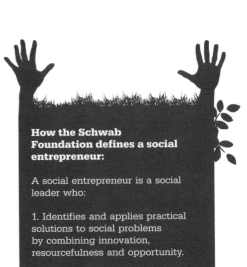

Social entrepreneurs, just like business entrepreneurs, are people who harness their creativity and resourcefulness to *create sustainable solutions* to the problems and needs that they see around them. Social entrepreneurs have a vision for a better future, and put their energy and skills into making something happen.

Within the idea of *social entrepreneurship*, there is also the idea of *social invention* – coming up with *innovative ideas* which can be used to address social problems. Not every social entrepreneur is an innovator; some will take other people's good ideas as their starting point. Not every social inventor is an entrepreneur; some will create ideas which have the potential to change the world, and then leave it to others to run with them.

Finally, there is the idea of *social enterprise*, creating enterprises which have both social and commercial goals – a sort of "double bottom line". Many social entrepreneurs develop enterprising solutions for generating resources to fund their projects, but many of these projects do not have any commercial viability.

These three terms share a common concept – *investing in individuals* and their ideas as an effective and highly efficient way of creating change, rather than supporting projects and programmes run by established organizations.

How the Schwab Foundation defines a social entrepreneur:

A social entrepreneur is a social leader who:

1. Identifies and applies practical solutions to social problems by combining innovation, resourcefulness and opportunity.

2. Innovates by finding a new product, a new service, or a new approach to a social problem.

3. Focuses first and foremost on social value creation and in that spirit, is willing to share openly the innovations and insights of the initiative with a view to its wider replication.

4. Doesn't wait to secure the resources before undertaking the catalytic innovation.

5. Is fully accountable to the constituencies s/he serves.

6. Resists being trapped by the constraints of ideology or discipline.

7. Continuously refines and adapts approach in response to feedback.

8. Has a vision, but also a well-thought out roadmap as to how to attain the goal.

Some organizations supporting social entrepreneurs

The **Ashoka Foundation**, founded by Bill Drayton in 1980, has been a pioneer in the field of social entrepreneurship. In countries all around the world, Ashoka seeks to identify social entrepreneurs and then offers them fellowships, support and networking with others doing similar things to help them succeed. Ashoka believes that the exceptional qualities they are looking for are found in around one person per annum per 10 million population. So there will be thirty people each year in the USA and six in the UK who have what it takes. Ashoka currently works in over sixty countries and is supporting over 1,800 fellows.

www.ashoka.org

www.changemakers.net

"**Social entrepreneurs are not content just to give a fish or teach how to fish. They will not rest until they have revolutionized the fishing industry.**"

Bill Drayton

UnLtd is a foundation which supports social entrepreneurs in the UK. It provides "have-a-go" awards to around 1,000 people a year (with a separately run youth programme supporting another 2,000 young people aged 11–25). UnLtd encourages anyone and everyone who feels that they have potential to do something for their communities or to create a better world. UnLtd supports individuals, not organizations or projects. A Level 1 award provides up to £5,000 towards project costs; a Level 2 award offers bursaries (mostly for one year, but sometimes for a longer period) for people to develop their ideas further.

www.unltd.org.uk

The **Skoll Foundation** was created in 1999 by Jeff Skoll, the first employee and first President of eBay. The Foundation makes awards for social entrepreneurship. These three-year awards support the continuation, replication or extension of programmes that have already proved their success. The Foundation has established the Skoll Centre at the Said Oxford Business School where it organizes an international conference for social entrepreneurs each year. It has also established Social Edge, an online community for sharing ideas and resources:

www.skollfoundation.org

www.socialedge.org

The **Schwab Foundation**, founded by Klaus Schwab, the creator of the World Economic Forum held each year at Davos, seeks to raise the profile of social entrepreneurship, offers Social Entrepreneur of the Year awards and provides access for social entrepreneurs to business and political networks.

www.schwabfound.org

The **School for Social Entrepreneurs** provides action learning for people to put their ideas into practice. It was founded by Michael Young, who created the Open University and the Consumers' Association. SSE is establishing a network of local schools to promote and support social entrepreneurship across the UK.

www.sse.org.uk

Over the next four pages, we show how four quite different people became social entrepreneurs and what they have been able to achieve.

LET THEM EAT FRUIT

The person: *Eric Samuel*, 47, was born in St Vincent in the Caribbean and brought up in St Albans near London. He had a career in banking, before being ordained a Pentecostal minister.

The starting point: Eric became interested in food poverty whilst doing a dissertation for his theology degree. He was living in Newham, one of the poorest neighbourhoods in Britain, where there was no ready access to shops or supermarkets to buy fresh fruit and vegetables affordably.

The problem: These neighbourhoods were "food deserts". Living there on low incomes meant an unhealthy diet, which led to obesity and other health problems.

The solution: To make fresh produce available at affordable prices, and to encourage healthier eating.

The first steps: Eric went to the Spitalfields wholesale market at 4.00 a.m. and purchased a car-load of fresh produce. He then sold this to local people at cost plus a 10 per cent mark up to recover his own costs. Eric sold the produce as cheaply as possible, to encourage people to buy. He then organized his customers into a food co-op.

What happened: Within one year, Eric was supplying six food co-ops, thirteen fruit tuckshops at local schools and three school breakfast clubs. He had established the Newham Food Access Partnership to promote food access and healthy eating across the borough.

Where next: Eric next set up Community Food Enterprise to run training programmes for health workers and "cook and eat" sessions for local residents. Eric became a national expert on food access, diet and poverty with first-hand knowledge of both the problems and the solutions. His next big idea is to set up Juice Bars in schools to be run as social enterprises by the students – promoting enterprise skills as well as a healthier eating.

The key: Just going out and doing it. Eric didn't have a salary to start with, any grants, or even a business plan. What he did have was a good idea for addressing a very real problem, the support of his family, free office space provided by a local charity and an infectious enthusiasm. This was all he needed.

Recognition: Eric won an award for best practice in community-led regeneration and became the UK "Volunteer of the Year" in 2001. Since then, he has continued to win accolades for his work on food poverty, and in 2006 was awarded a MBE in the Queen's Birthday Honours.

NEWHAM FOOD ACCESS PARTNERSHIP:
www.nfap.org.uk

COMMUNITY FOOD ENTERPRISE:
www.community-food-enterprise.org.uk

FEED THEIR MINDS, FEED THEIR FUTURES

The person: *Asha Mehta,* 70, wife of Mahendra, a retired Mumbai (Bombay) diamond merchant and Rotarian.

The starting point: Asha and Mahendra set up the Ratna Nidhi Charitable Trust in the 1980s. Asha feeds children, Mahendra provides vocational training for disadvantaged youth and runs health camps in South Asia and Africa.

The problem: To find a way of encouraging children to attend school regularly.

The solution: The Food for Education programme works with nurseries and schools. The children get breakfast to start their day with and then a nutritious meal after their schooling. Being fed properly increases concentration, improves health, and provides an opportunity for social interaction whilst eating. The results are significantly higher levels of attendance and improved learning.

The Food for Saving programme reaches street and working children attending non-formal education centres. The children contribute a minimum of Rs2 for their meal (about 5 US cents), which is put into a savings account. After one year they can use their savings as they wish.

The first steps: Asha based her operation at her old family residence in Bombay Central. Support came from the family trust and friends. She set up a production line to prepare and deliver the food daily, and now employs three kitchen staff and two drivers. The food is delivered by rickshaw in large containers; empty containers from the previous day are collected.

What happened: Asha is feeding 3,000 children each day for 225 school days each year, plus 2,000 street and working children for six days a week throughout the year.

Where next: Asha also recycles and distributes clothing to the poor, and imports around 100,000 educational and general knowledge books which are distributed to schools and libraries throughout India.

The key: Asha is not trying to change the whole world. But with a lot of effort and some creativity, she is having a profound impact on children's lives. Helping them attend and do better at school gives them a better chance for the future.

Recognition: Asha, none to date. Mahendra has a Rotary lifetime achievement award.

RATNA NIDHI CHARITABLE TRUST:
www.rnct.org

HELPING STREET CHILDREN IN CRISIS

The person: *Jeroo Billimoria*, 30, a faculty member at Tata Institute of Social Sciences, Mumbai (Bombay), India's leading postgraduate social work training institute.

The starting point: TISS had been offered a freephone number – 10-9-8 – by the Indian telecoms service to launch a crisis helpline for children in need. Jeroo's students were expected to do a field action project as part of their degree.

The problem: Street children are vulnerable to physical and sexual abuse, have health and drug problems through living and working on the streets, and are often exploited by employers and even the police.

The solution: To set up a free telephone line for dealing with crisis situations. The line would be manned 24/7 by volunteer workers and street children on a rota basis, and each call responded to with practical assistance as required.

The first steps: Jeroo approached four organizations working with street children in different areas of Greater Mumbai and persuaded them to offer her facilities for running a telephone helpline within their programme. The phone company would route the 10-9-8 call to the nearest centre.

What happened: the children's problems were dealt with, and Jeroo showed that the service was both needed and effective.

Where next: Jeroo met a guest speaker at TISS who helped her design a replication strategy for starting the service in other cities, draw up a business plan, and win a grant from the UK lottery. The idea was to expand into six other cities. At this stage the Government of India became interested, and provided support. Within three years, the service had reached fifty-eight cities across India. Jeroo then organized an international conference and set up Child Helpline International (based in the Netherlands) to promote children's helplines across the world.

The key: An empathy with the children, and a child-centred approach (children would be returned to their families or given a room in a hostel only if *they* wished this); the ambition to develop the project nationally right from the start; getting the support of UNICEF (to pay for training), the Government of India and Tata Consultancy Services (to design an IT system to keep records and control an operation spread across a vast country); the loyal support of her students, some of whom became staff of the NGO that she set up.

Recognition: Jeroo was awarded an Ashoka Fellowship, and in 2006 received a Skoll award to develop her next project called Aflatoun to promote children's banking.

www.childlineindia.org.in

www.childhelplineinternational.org

www.aflatoun.org

PROMOTING ENTERPRISE SKILLS IN THE TOWNSHIPS

The person: *Taddy Blecher,* 33, a successful actuary working in Johannesburg.

The starting point: In 1995 Taddy was offered a job in the USA. At the very last moment, he changed his mind, and spent the next five years in Alexandra and Soweto townships, helping school kids matriculate. It was in 2000 that he was ready to take the next step.

The problem: Students were telling Taddy that they could not afford tertiary education and they couldn't get jobs.

The solution: Taddy came up with the idea of a Business School for township students. Students would take the skills they acquired back to townships and rural areas and create businesses that would give them a livelihood. Students would pay just 7 per cent of an equivalent course in another institution, but would contribute to the running of the

college by helping with cleaning, computer maintenance and administration.

The first steps: Taddy was offered a building to house his CIDA City Campus. He enrolled 250 students. But he still had no money, no equipment, no materials. Taddy, with his self-help approach and the volunteer help that he could mobilize, designed and ran courses that met the students' needs and went on to establish an "alternative business school" of which he is the President.

What happened: By 2005, CIDA had 1,300 students, owned four downtown buildings (all donated), had books worth R100 million and 1,400 computers.

Where next: In 2003 the CIDA Information Technology Academy was opened, which now has 321 students. CIDA ConnectLab has trained 1,500 call centre workers from Soweto and Diepkloof (the call centre company was donated). CIDA opened in Cape Town in 2005, and there are plans to set up in KwaZulu-Natal and Eastern Cape.

The key: Taddy had a dream, and did not think about the problems, but just set about turning that dream into reality. He had "an unbelievable passion, love and excitement for what CIDA was doing . . . 'What I do is *not work*'". He developed skills, like public speaking, as he went along. He was able to bring in business support and get employees to volunteer. He claims 280 innovations which have enabled the venture to succeed. Alumni students once earning now contribute to help pay for the next generation of students.

Recognition: Taddy won the Global Leader of Tomorrow Award from the World Economic Forum in 2002 and again in 2005.

www.cida.co.za

BOOKS TO INSPIRE YOU

The world needs you and your ideas! But if you are not yet convinced about this, then here are twelve books you should read:

War and peace:

A Dirty War: a Russian Reporter in Chechnya, by Anna Politkovskaya. This is a warts and all account of what a conflict zone is really like. Anna was murdered in 2006 as a result of her fearless journalism.

The Dressing Station: a Surgeon's Odyssey, by Jonathan Caplan. A young South African doctor travels to war zones and becomes an expert in trauma surgery.

We Wish to Inform You That Tomorrow We Will Be Killed with Our Families, stories from the Rwandan genocide by Philip Gourevitch.

Healthy living:

Where there is No Doctor, one of a range of manuals for village health workers which have been published across the world by the Hesperian Foundation. This book will help you understand how lucky we are to have access to doctors, hospitals and medicines.

Not on the Label: What Really Goes into the Food on Your Plate, by Felicity Lawrence. This book will change the way you eat!

The world's environment under stress:

An Inconvenient Truth, by Al Gore. Sets out the case for action on global warming. If you don't want to read the book, watch the Oscar-winning film.

High Tide: news from a warming world, by Mark Lynas. Reports from some of the world's global-warming hotspots where climate change is happening.

When the Rivers Run Dry: What Happens When Our Water Runs Out, by Fred Pearce. Water will become a hugely important issue for the survival of the world as we know it.

International development:

Everybody Loves a Good Drought: Stories from India's Poorest Districts, by P. Sainath. A journalist visits some of the most backward communities and explores the development process in practice.

The Human Development Report published annually by the United Nations, with all the facts on poverty and inequality that you will ever need.

The end of the world:

The Doomsday Book: Scenarios for the End of the World, by Joel Levy. From an asteroid impact, to superbugs and nanotechnology out of control, this book examines all the threats facing the very future of the planet, and assesses their likelihood and seriousness.

Worldchanging, all the issues of the world between two covers with examples of what people are doing about them – which might just avert the doomsday scenario.

And when you've bought and read each book, register it on BookCrossing and leave it around for someone else to read . . . who will then pass it on to someone else:

www.bookcrossing.com

If you would like to recommend a book for others to read, go to **www.365act.com**

Put the books that have inspired you on **www.librarything.com** so that they can inspire others. Create a link between your website and your *LibraryThing* page.

ATTEND TO YOUR OWN WELLBEING

Before you start to change the world, make sure that you are fit to do so. You don't want to drop dead with your efforts still incomplete! You need to be alive, alert and healthy.

Here are ten simple steps to take:

1. **Make sure you have a healthy heart.** Check your body mass index to see if you are at risk of heart disease or a stroke. If you're overweight, do something about it. **www.worldheartday.com/aheartforlife/ obesity.asp**

2. **Get health checked** from time to time (especially as you get older). Get screened for cancer as your doctor recommends. Keep up to date on your vaccinations (and inoculations if you travel abroad).

3. **Don't guzzle pills** for things like colds and headaches, unless you are in extreme discomfort. Your body has its own ways of making things better.

4. **Eat healthily.** Give up supplements and stop being a junk food junkie. Have a balanced diet. Remember *it's five-a-day* for fruit and veg (that's five portions).

5. **Eat less meat;** explore the idea of becoming a vegetarian. This will also be good for the environment.

6. **Give up smoking.** If you are a smoker, then STOP. Give it up today. Right now! You'll be saving your life as well as your lungs, and you'll be making life healthier and more comfortable for everyone around you.

7. **Walk or ride a bike** whenever you can, instead of driving. This will be good for you and reduce congestion for those who need to go by car.

8. **Take exercise.** If you don't play sport or go to a gym, then at least walk up the stairs, rather than taking the lift (for the first few floors at least). Walk up the escalators at Underground stations.

9. **Get yourself tested for STDs and AIDS** if you feel you are at risk. Make sure that you or your partner is wearing a condom if and whenever you should.

10. **Smile; do something for others; give money to charity.** Happy philanthropists live longer. That's a proven fact!

THINGS TO DO FOR SPECIAL OCCASIONS

There are the officially designated days which draw attention to an issue in today's world. For example:

World Press Freedom Day, 3 May. Press freedom is an important contributor to a functioning democracy and the elimination of corruption and cronyism. More than a third of the world's population live in countries where there is no freedom to report what is happening and journalists are persecuted for telling the truth. Find out about press abuse and campaign to get imprisoned journalists and writers freed. Reporters without Borders campaigns for journalists:

www.rsf.org

PEN campaigns for writers:

www.internationalpen.org.

International Day for Biological Diversity, 22 May. This day allows us to reflect on the importance of preserving the planet's genetic heritage for future generations. Whilst you are doing this, why not grow seeds for poor farmers to enable them to plant their gardens and fields. The Kokopelli Seed Foundation is a worldwide network of seed-growers who contribute their seeds to a seed fund for poor farmers in developing countries. Grow tomatoes, pumpkins, peppers, pulses, carrots and produce seeds for Kokopelli.

www.kokopelli-seeds.com

World Environment Day, 5 June. Do something to draw attention to the importance of sustaining the world's environment on which we all depend. Do one thing. Join a demonstration, borrow a friend's bicycle and learn to ride it, plant a tree, collect old books and send them for recycling, join a Freecycling group, change all the bulbs at home to low energy, switch to green electricity. Click on "Events" at:

www.unep.org. If you want to do more, there are also two Earth Days (around 20 March and on 22 April).

Human Rights Day, 10 December; or Ang San Suu Kyi's birthday, 19 June. Ang San Suu Kyi is opposition leader in Burma, and kept under house arrest. The fact that she won a free election is conveniently forgotten. She also won the 1991 Nobel Peace Prize. Send a birthday card to Aung Saan Suu Kyi. Send it to 612 K Street NW, Suite 401, Washington DC 20006. If you want to do more, then arrest yourself for Burma Day in your own house. Invite your friends to stay over for twenty-four hours. Have a good time. Tell the media.

www.uscampaignforburma.org

Find out about all the days, weeks, years and decades that have been specially designated by the United Nations that highlight an issue or commemorate an event.

www.unac.org/en/news_events/un_days/international_days.asp

There are seasons which can be marked by doing something special (the longest day, the shortest day, the planting season . . . there are also public holidays such as Christmas and Ramadan where giving is encouraged.

St Valentine's Day, 14 February. This year do something unusual for your loved one. Buy a conflict-free diamond. A Global Witness guide tells you the questions to ask the jeweller to ensure that what you buy is conflict free. Check out: **www.globalwitness.org**

Send charity flowers (in the UK)
www.charityflowers.co.uk

. . . or an organic bouquet (in the USA)
www.organicbouquet.com

World Ocean Day, 8 June. Ocean environments around the world are under severe stress, due to rising sea temperatures, overfishing, destruction of coral reefs, the impact of cruise ships, entangled animals, marine debris, pollution, mercury contamination, offshore drilling, unsustainable coastal development and many other factors. The basic problem is humankind's greed and unconcern for what is a common resource. Pledge to do two things. Stop eating endangered fish. Check out fish to avoid and to eat with a clear conscience at **www.fishonline.org**.

Participate in the the *International Coastal Cleanup*, which takes place in September each year – 300,000 volunteers in 90 countries clean up over 11,000 miles of shoreline:
www.coastalcleanup.org.

World Ocean Day: **www.theoceanproject.org**

Feed the Birds Day is the last Saturday in October, when the clocks go back to winter time. This is the time of year when garden birds really need help to get them through the rigours of the upcoming winter. The Royal Society for the Protection of Birds has advice on attracting birds into your garden, feeding them and even on green bird food.
www.rspb.org.uk/feedthebirds

Buy Nothing Day, the day after Thanksgiving (USA and Canada) which is the fourth Thursday in November; elsewhere, the day after that. It is celebrated in fifty-five countries to draw attention to the excesses of a consumer society. It is a day "when you can turn the economy off and talk about it". Make sure that you buy absolutely nothing. Don't spend a single penny.
www.ecoplan.org/ibnd/ib_index.htm and **www.buynothingday.co.uk.**

There's even a **Buy Nothing Christmas** started by Canadian Mennonites with the aim of regaining the essential spirit of Christmas: **www.buynothingchristmas.org**

You could also resolve to change the world on **New Year's Day** (1 January) as your New Year's Resolution. Celebrate **TV Turnoff Day** (late April) by turning off your TV and doing something more useful.
www.turnoffyourtv.com.

On **Guy Fawkes Day** (5 November) you could make a commitment to change the world by non-violent means.

Find out about specially designated days that you've never heard of – such as **National Dog Biscuit Day** and **Internet-Free Day.** Think of something to do to celebrate the day, which will also benefit the world.

Check out the calendar at:
http://homeschooling.about.com/od/ fundaycalendars/index_a.htm

Or why not designate your own day to highlight whatever your cause is? Whether it is Internet spam or green funerals, there's a date just waiting to be chosen by you!

NOW YOU CAN BECOME AN EVERYDAY ACTIVIST

A CALL TO ACTION

Right, you've read the book. You've been inspired by some really interesting people who are doing really interesting things, there are issues and problems you really care about, and you've decided to take that crucial first step. Now's the time to get going on changing the world!

Pledge to make a difference

I pledge to become an *everyday activist* and really make a difference

This is the issue that I'm going to do something about:

_____

_____

This is what I'm going to do:

_____

_____

_____

_____

This is the first step I'm going to take:

_____

_____

_____

_____

Signed: _____   Date:_____

Next turn your pledge into action. Become an *everyday activist*. Good luck. All success with your attempt to change the world.

Tell us about your ideas and your achievements.
Write to 365@civa.org.uk and visit www.365act.com